Invisible Citizens

Invisible Citizens

Youth Politics After September 11

Edited by
Ganesh Sitaraman and Previn Warren

Assistant Editors

Sean Creehan   Jim Kruzer
Miranda Dugi   Riley Mendoza
John Ellison   Swati Mylavarapu
Ilan Graff   Geoff Reed
Ashley Isaacson   Patrick Toomey
Joseph Jackson

With Funding from The Institute of Politics

iUniverse, Inc.
New York Lincoln Shanghai

Invisible Citizens
Youth Politics After September 11

iUniverse, Inc.

For information address:
iUniverse
2021 Pine Lake Road, Suite 100
Lincoln, NE 68512
www.iuniverse.com

ISBN: 0-595-27106-5

Printed in the United States of America

For

M.W. & H.C

T.J. & M.K.G.

Table of Contents

Preface

This book tells the tale of America's largest untapped body of voters and what happened to them after one of the greatest crises in national history. Young people aged 18-25 have generally been considered a lost cause by politicians, policymakers, and many political scientists. We are viewed as a disinterested, relatively self-absorbed community, a perception buoyed by our consistently low voter turnouts and the media-crafted representation of young people as glib, sarcastic, and apathetic. But while voting records state an irrefutable reality, it is too often assumed that the cause of low turnout is indeed some kind of jaded youth culture of irony. This conclusion is patently false. Young people are some of the most active members of their communities and are devoting increasing amounts of their time to direct service work and volunteerism. The question before September 11, to those few academics bold enough to care, was why young people had not translated this activism in the realm of service into a subsequent engagement in politics.

For a moment, September 11 seemed to resolve this question neatly, or at least allow the issue to be conveniently tabled. This was it, at long last–a defining moment for our generation, a Pearl Harbor for Generation X. The size and magnitude of the event seemed to unite young people into a determinedly patriotic (but diverse and fiercely independent) bundle, poised to tackle the national problems of the next millennium. Of course, this kind of sentimental, optimistic account is not readily proffered a year after the event, but not because it has been replaced by anything more realistic or sensible. Rather, it seems that pundits, journalists, and, far more disturbingly, our national leaders, have used this trope as a way of dismissing the need to address what still remains one of the most disturbing and crucial questions facing our nation's political future: why aren't young people engaged in the political process, and what can be done about it?

It is not the goal of this book to offer a comprehensive answer to that question, but rather to stimulate a new inquiry into the very question by exposing just how critical the issue of youth engagement still is. September 11 presented policymakers, educators, and journalists with a crucial opportunity to reconnect with America's youth, but it is a window of opportunity that is closing and closing fast. In the wake of the tragedy, young people showed significantly higher levels of awareness and interest in the political process and in national and international affairs. Between October 2000 and October 2001, polls reported a 14% jump in the level of students' trust towards the federal government.[i] Between October 2001 and October 2002, however, trust fell by 9%. Half as many students reported participating in a government, political, or issues-oriented group in October 2002 as they had immediately after the tragedies. Across the board, students' levels of engagement with the political process between 2000 and 2002 show a distinct but sharp spike, from which we are currently coming down. It won't be long before our levels of political participation look as low, or lower, than they were before the attacks.

This, of course, is no real news to young people themselves. In May 2002, a survey of college-aged Americans found that "71% do not expect to see a long term continuation of recent increases in patriotism and national unity."[ii] Youth have generally either ignored or dismissed clarion calls from pundits heralding in a new, refocused generation. Most young people are hardly willing to consider the government theirs, let alone take its helm; the same May 2002 survey found that a majority of youth tend to talk about government as "the" government rather than "our" government.[iii] But as we have noted, this is indifference born of something besides sheer apathy. It seems to be a conscious, voluntary response–a deliberate turning-away from a process that has turned its backs on young people. It is difficult to locate cause and effect here; politicians are as likely to claim that they don't target the youth vote because youth "don't care" as are young people apt to decry a political system that ignores or marginalizes their concerns. Rather than solve this chicken-and-egg problem, we must examine the underlying reasons from which this double-bind has arisen.

The culprit, it turns out, is not "young people" or "politicians," but certain broader characteristics of our political system at the beginning of the twenty-first century. Young people, like many citizens in general, feel an increasing gulf separating themselves from the decisions being made by their leaders. Young people in particular have been routinely denied ready access to legitimate information about politics, through the steady trivialization of television news content and the atrophying of public school civics curricula. Perhaps as importantly, they have experienced less and less face time with their government. 62% of people under 30 say they were never asked to consider working in government while they were in high school or college.[iv] 78% claim that their fellow students are not well informed about programs such as AmeriCorps, VISTA, and the Peace Corps, arguably some of the most effective means of directly bringing young people into the realm of public service.[v] In short, young people are not approaching politics because politics is failing to approach them. Without this crucial connection, they have been left to interpret the worst aspects of modern political culture as indicative of what government is and how it must operate. The troubling preponderance of corporate money in political campaigns, a recurring dependence among politicians on negative advertising, and a trend among politicians to follow polls rather than lead through vision are all common stereotypes of the political process among young people. They are stereotypes precisely because they are true. But what young people have failed to realize is that these are not constitutive standards of politics–not "business as usual"–but raw, offensive abnormalities that must be addressed and challenged. In doing so, the importance of political service would be affirmed rather than forgotten, the project of government salvaged rather than dismissed. Those in power are understandably not keen on allowing us to make this link.

The goal of this book is to show how September 11 did or did not affect a change in the landscape of youth attitudes towards politics. Measuring such change must take into account more than just empirical findings. While survey data can provide a general sense of how patterns have shifted, they tend to obscure the subtleties of an issue as staggeringly complex as encompassing "generational attitudes." Young people are not a monolithic entity. For that reason, a bulk of the book explores the impact of September 11 on political engagement through personal anecdotes, memoirs, and narratives. The stories of the young Americans in this book reflect a constellation of different political orientations, backgrounds, and viewpoints. At the same time, they give evidence to a number of noticeable trends, which are mirrored in quantitative survey data.

Our qualitative research is placed in the framework of various topical analyses, each of which highlights the change in youth awareness regarding a specific aspect of social and political life after September 11. Chapter One, "Ruby Tuesday," looks at the immediate emotional impact of September 11 on young people, demonstrating just how much the attacks influenced our consciousness. Chapter Two, "A Generation Responds," considers the extent to which this emotional impact can be translated into a political impact. Although 9/11 caused a spike in awareness, which manifested itself through increased patriotism and short-term participation, increased awareness was neither permanent nor translated into action and engagement. Chapters Three, Four, and Five address issues related to homeland security, the U.S. military, and international affairs. Each demonstrates the increase in awareness after September 11, but likewise shows the tentative nature of our shift in civic spirit. Increased trust and participation are intertwined with our ingrained belief in the "dirty" and ineffective culture of politics. Finally, the conclusion provides tangible ways in which policymakers can inspire our generation to higher levels of civic engagement.

This book was developed with the help of Harvard University's Institute of Politics. The institute, created as a living tribute to John F. Kennedy, is the nation's largest nonpartisan undergraduate political organization, and seeks to inspire young people to careers in politics and public service. With the help of the Institute, we worked with eleven other students to contact scores of young people across the United States and to gather their insights and perspectives on politics, government, and civic and social life after September 11.

In addition to these individual memoirs, we drew extensively on three nationwide surveys conducted by the Institute between 2000 and 2002. The surveys sought to illuminate the attitudes that America's youth hold towards politics and public service, and in the process provided a wealth of information on the collective psyche of our generation. The text of the 2002 Institute of Politics survey is included as an appendix.

We began writing this book in January 2002 and hardly expected it to change as much as it did in the next four months. But throughout the writing and rewriting, we were unconditionally supported by a few amazing individuals who were always able and willing to help: former Clinton administration terrorism expert, Juliette Kayyem; political advertising genius, Bill Hillsman; and Institute of Politics Outreach Director Gordon Li. They consistently provided excellent guidance, advice, and support along every step of the way, and never hesitated to tell us their candid opinions however much we may or may not have wanted to hear them. We would also like to thank the staff of the Institute of Politics, especially Senator David Pryor, Secretary Dan Glickman, Cathy McLaughlin, and the Institute's Student Advisory Committee. Without the Institute's help, this book could never have been written.

We would like to thank Sean Creehan, Miranda Dugi, John Ellison, Ilan Graff, Ashley Isaacson, Joseph Jackson, Jim Kruzer, Riley Mendoza, Swati Mylavarapu, Geoff Reed, and Patrick Toomey. These eleven hard-working and brilliant fellow students not only pushed us to define our objectives and clarify our purpose but also acted as the driving force in collecting much of the book's content. This book is as much as anything a testament to their labors and insights.

From before we started writing, three of our friends, Erin Ashwell, Peter Buttigieg, and Ryan Rippel, were unqualified enthusiasts. Their spirit and excitement, not to mention their providential counsel, guided us during innumerable times of difficulty and propelled us further than we imagined.

During our research, we had the pleasure to speak with many people about American politics and generational identity, including Professor Sidney Verba, Professor Robert Putnam, Professor Samuel P. Huntington, Ambassador Jonathan Moore, and Senator Chuck Robb. Each provided important insights that afforded us with much food for thought.

Additionally, we would like to thank Rick Kaplan, whose experience and guidance were invaluable, Ceci Connolly, who read early sections and helped solidify our conceptual framework, and Matt Bai, whose feedback was incredibly helpful. We'd also like to thank Larry Harris, Erin Ross, Jesse Levey, and Jack Schnirman of United Leaders; Bill Burke-White, Heather Quay, Sven H. Ingrape, and Kevin Scully.

We have special thanks to our parents and families. They are eternally understanding, and in the hardest and easiest times alike, they fully support our endeavors.

Finally, we would like to thank the many students who contributed their illuminating perspectives, heartfelt recollections, and candid opinions to the book. We were constantly impressed, often surprised, and always appreciative of their hard work and willingness to share.

Ganesh Sitaraman & Previn Warren
Cambridge, MA
February 2003

Chapter 1:

Ruby Tuesday

Few remember September 10, 2001. A glance at the calendar tells us it was a Monday. According to the newspapers, President Bush stood in the Washington Navy Yard early in the morning, offering commemorative remarks at a ceremony with the Prime Minister of Australia. Congress, looking forward to a busy week, anticipated important votes on defense authorization and minimum wage legislation. The Dow Jones Industrial Average closed at 9,605 after a day of moderate trading. And the Yankees had traveled to Boston, where Roger Clemens prepared to garner a twentieth victory against his former team in the final contest of a four-game series.

But the game never happened. Not because improvised missiles pierced the symbols of American economic and military prowess. Not because Americans had been wrenched from their everyday lives to witness assault, terror, and death. Not because the world had changed. The Red Sox-Yankees match was simply washed out, cancelled due to rain and unplayable field conditions. But who, besides maybe Roger, remembers that?

September 10 can be reconstructed from an impersonal record. With a bit of research, we can describe and detail that typically bland Monday according to the usual measures–stock market performance, presidential appearances, sports schedules. But no one can actually remember it. It is as if recollection of that day has been sequestered in some remote corner of our memories. But proceed one day further along the September calendar and a personal history pours forth from the mouth of even the most reticent observer.

More than a laundry list of generic facts, the history of September 11 must be conceived as a web of narratives–the common project of 280 million separate stories. Though we witnessed tragedy together in real-time, our memories convey a diversity of struggles and reactions. The accounts of our respondents echo this tension. One Columbia student, only miles north of Ground Zero at the time, describes:

> I experienced the madness through CNN just like the rest of the world did. I had learned about the attacks and seen the mass incident unfold on TV just as my family saw the same thing in Buenos Aires. I realized that the experience of September 11 was shared nationwide and worldwide. The WTC attacks happened to all of us. We all went through the same horror.

Another New York student tells us, however, that "what September 11 most left me with was the notion that September 11, 2001 does not mean the same thing for everyone." As always, we are left with many questions. How did this multiplicity of meanings emerge out of a day experienced in common? What does it mean to participate in the horror of tragedy? And what rituals of closure can translate the impulses of panic, grief, and anger into new and lasting resolutions? But what occupies this chapter is one simple truth: everyone can recall their September 11. Before all else, then, we shall examine September 11 as a day of emotion, implicitly subjective and etched in memory by the crude force of catastrophe.

History as an academic discipline must constantly call upon both established fact and individual account to reconstruct the past. The events of September 11 may be arranged chronologically, fixed as fact, and offered neatly inside a box. But this chapter seeks to offer a different sort of history. Our history is subjective–full of fragments, interrupted glimpses, and unexpected discontinuities that enrich its meaning. Our history rests on narrations not facts; it is situated in the particulars of individual lives that together comprise the collective horror of a nation and the first reaction of a generation. A history of this type is one that does not presume to judge and cannot hope to exclude. It is a democratic history, a history of countless perspectives, experiences, and reflections; a history which lives at every point where the events of that day have carved memory out of emotion, hope, or suffering. A simple chronology establishes only the plane upon which millions of separate stories unfold–it is the common medium of these memories.

A subjective history of September 11 requires a healthy cross-section of individual recollections. Because the strongest memories are bound to powerful emotional associations, this historical project must begin with the intense sensations wrung from the twenty-four hours of September 11. The tragedy, panic, and confusion of September 11 gave every American his or her own memory of that day, whether by fear, shock, sorrow, or anger. Though the official death toll today rests at a horrifying three thousand lives, at least twice as many, and perhaps even tens of thousands, were predicted dead in the immediate aftermath of the attacks. Stranded above floors made impassable by fire, men and women jumped into a 110-story void, preferring this death to the one directly below. Even as the towers crumbled, rescue workers raced upward, floor by floor. Mothers frantically dialed and redialed their sons and daughters. Our President appeared on the run, hurriedly ushered from one secure site to the next. The rest of us sat motionless in front of our televisions, watching the dust hungrily consume lower Manhattan.

In those moments of emotion, America half-grasped a new vulnerability. The identity of our attackers remained uncertain, but the calculated evil of such an assault upon the comfortable certainties of everyday life could not be mistaken. One respondent compares the day to December 7, 1941. And she is correct–like Pearl Harbor, September 11 is "a day that will live in infamy." Carved into history for its deep wickedness, unfathomable tragedy, and profound revision of our nation's course, this day will not recede into obscurity. But let us remember that September 11 will live first and foremost in the memories of those who lived through it. That day has etched our memories with emotions as hard as facts. History, in truth, thrives equally in the minds of spectators and the books of commentators.

What then shall we make of September 10? It stands not merely as the day that naively anticipated September 11: it has come to signify all the days-before. Since the attacks, philosopher-pundits have divided the history of our generation's consciousness into two great eras: before and after September 11. But the effects of this tragedy cannot be so readily resolved and set aside. In many ways, the mission of *this* book is confrontation: it acknowledges a struggle to define the meaning of an event in its aftermath. Looking to young Americans, it tests the simplistic assumptions about September 11 that have uncritically been accepted by popular wisdom.

The emotions created by September 11 created memories–this point is unquestionable. But the arranging of memories is the first step toward inventing meaning. What and how we remember will guide our response to these events far beyond the prayer vigils, the anniversaries, and the war on terrorism. The student accounts included in this book suggest how emotion can be translated into an intellectual awareness that animates a generation. They must be our starting point.

Lauren, age 24
Washington, D.C.
Editorial Assistant, "The Hotline"

At 8:55 a.m. on September 11, I looked up at a television above my desk to see what everyone in the office was talking about. I was watching, confused like everyone else, when the second plane hit the south tower. I work in the news business. Breaking news is what gets me going. The rush, the horror, the sheer intensity excite me. But this story was different. This story was mine...my friends'...my family's.

Being in Washington, I felt detached from everything that was happening. The real action, the real tragedy was in New York, but I felt just as terrorized. And I felt numb. Rumors abounded...a car bomb on the Mall; another plane headed to the Capitol; four planes still unaccounted for in the air; fires all around the city. Michael Bay would have a hit with this movie, I remember thinking.

My parents were vacationing in San Francisco, and knowing they would not be awake yet, I called their hotel room and woke up my dad. I could picture him turning to the alarm clock when I asked him if he knew anyone in the World Trade Center, seeing it was 6 a.m., and I knew his answer–"Not this early"–did not take the time difference into account. I called my cousin, who I knew worked in finance and in Manhattan. I had no idea where his office was located.

Only bits and pieces from the next few days remain clear. The afternoon of September 11 I spent in a bar. It was 2 p.m., and the bar was full. In fact, we tried two bars before that one, and both were standing room only. But I understood. I didn't want to go home either, to watch television alone. No one knew what else would happen that day, and somehow the idea of being with a group of people–even people I didn't know–seemed better than being alone.

That night I went to a friend's house to watch the news. Her apartment building has a rooftop patio, from which we could see the smoke still billowing from the Pentagon. And we ordered a pizza. We watched CNN, and smoked, and ate pizza.

My colleague's father passed away in mid-August, and she told me just a few days after September 11 that she was glad her dad did not live to see that day. He lived through the day that will live in infamy, she said. For me, and I think for my generation, it is this day, 9/11, that will invoke the same kind of horror and sadness as December 7, 1941. It will live within me forever.

Sometime in October, a friend and I were talking about when life would go back to normal. This is normal now. Normal has changed.

Sarah, age 20
Fort Valley, Virginia
University of Virginia

I was debriefed while making what I thought was my normal trek to class up Rugby Road the morning of September 11. I bumped into a friend who delivered the news: a plane had crashed into the World Trade Center. I did not even begin to imagine the far-reaching significance this tragedy would have in the days, weeks, and months to come. But I knew I had to get to a TV.

Detached and oblivious to all else as the breaking story unfolded, I watched as my world of security and certainty vanished into the thick black smoke. Despite the fact that I've been to the top of the Empire State Building, seen "Cats" on Broadway, and ice skated in Central Park, New York City seemed a million miles away from the small city of Charlottesville, Virginia. Watching the Twin Towers crumble was surreal. Looking at the four sided Pentagon was shocking. It was like watching "Armageddon" or "Independence Day," movies that spent millions of dollars trying to evoke even a fraction of the horror of September 11. Ironically, these movies made the reality of September 11 feel all the more devastating.

There were TVs in the dining halls, in the faculty lounges (where the faculty became lost among the hordes of curious students), in the classrooms, and in the halls. The world seemed to stop–the only thing moving was the picture on the television. Some professors canceled classes. Some offered their cell phones to students who urgently needed to contact a family member. Everyone showed compassion the likes of which I have never seen and may never see again.

A lot of people needed to talk about what happened. There were countless vigils and forums for students to grieve and reflect together. The Lawn glowed the whole night as candles made the Academic Village appear covered by a white blanket.

But for some reason, I could not bring myself to participate. I almost felt ridiculous for grieving. Although my country was devastated by a breach in national security, I was fine. My family was fine. The buildings themselves meant little to me and I did not know a soul inside. As I fell asleep the night of September 11, I could not stop thinking about the people whose lives were forever changed. The people who lost their mother or their husband or their best friend had the right to grieve—I did not.

The United States erected a newfound patriotism out of the rubble. The rebellion that characterized America's mood, prevalent since Vietnam, disappeared faster than the World Trade Center fell. Charlottesville, like every city in America, became crowded with American flags. Even today, Americans are almost unanimously in favor of the war against terrorism.

Nevertheless, the industry that grew out of patriotism alarms me. Ground Zero is now a district in New York City, wrought with T-shirt and hot dog vendors that cater to the mass amount of tourists gawking at the enormous graveyard. It does not seem right that the sight of such heroism and goodwill is now, six short months later, a money-making ploy. I see genuine patriotism giving way to lucrative advertising schemes. I see many of the people who seemed so distraught on September 11 not giving those events a passing thought today.

But I am sure those who felt the dust sting their eyes or smelled a body burning alive will never forget those images. Those who lost a loved one will probably not go a day without grieving. It is for those people I am sad. It is their grief I will never forget.

Jessica, age 21
Woodstock, Virginia
Columbia University, Studying at the American University in Cairo

On September 11 I was studying abroad at the American University in Cairo, Egypt. As I was walking out of my Arabic language class around 4pm (Cairo time) I decided to go to the cafeteria and get a snack. As I walked in I glanced at the cafeteria television and stopped dead in my tracks. There were two gaping, flaming holes in both World Trade Centers. A crowd had gathered around the television set but I couldn't understand what was going on because the news in Egypt is broadcast in Arabic, but the crowd around the television had already come to the consensus that it must have been an accident. I suddenly had a very nervous feeling that I should get to the hostel as soon as possible to call my family in America.

When I got back to the hostel I called my mother in Virginia. She answered the phone cheerily and asked me if I was having a good time in Egypt; it was a beautiful day and her azaleas were...*Mom turn on the TV!* I screamed, realizing she had no idea our nation was being attacked. For the next hour she relayed the news as best as she could–when it was reported that the Pentagon had been bombed we both began to cry. I was 7,000 miles away in a third-world nation known for its terrorist groups. All of the airports in the United States were closed. I couldn't go home.

For the next forty-eight hours I lived my life in a constant panic. I tried to call my friends in New York but the phones wouldn't work. The computers in the hostel crashed. The American embassy was evacuated. We were told there were celebrations in Cairo and that we should not leave the hostel. We left the hostel anyway because we thought it would be a target. The Americans in the hostel were disgusted and angry; some of the non-American Arabs in the hostel were defensive and antagonistic. Some Americans panicked and fled to Europe. I couldn't sleep at night because every time I shut my eyes there was a plane flying into my bedroom. Every slammed door was a bomb. When I entered a room I would immediately look for all the possible escape routes. After a few weeks, things quieted down and I made it through a night of sleep without waking up in a panic. The memory of watching people jump from the towers with a voice-over in Arabic will always remain in my memory. But the most poignant moment brought about by September 11 for me personally came two weeks after the catastrophe. I was reading a description in an American magazine of lower Manhattan on the day of the bombings. The magazine reported that the streets were littered with discarded high-heeled shoes, kicked off by women as they fled the carnage.

At that point I had lived in a Muslim country for almost a month. I was harassed daily for being an unveiled Western woman. I felt proud that our country tried to provide equality and safety for its women. But reading that magazine passage made me want to cry. I could not get the picture out of my mind–women running barefoot through flaming steel and jagged glass. Women who had "made it"–worked in the same prestigious offices as men and made the same salaries–but nonetheless could not run in an emergency. How many women died because they could not run? While the news was full of the images of women removing their *burqas* my mind was full of the screams of women as they ran barefoot through the smoldering chaos of lower Manhattan.

Rami, age 19
Mt. Prospect, Illinois
Georgetown University

I woke up too early…I had planned to wake up an hour before my 2:15 class across campus. Something was strange. I could hear people running—someone outside was yelling…not a typical college morning. Most mornings, the only thing you could hear was the chirping of the birds as students walked silently by like zombies to class. Something was definitely wrong with this particular Tuesday…I had strictly told my roommate not to bother me until the afternoon. For some reason, though, he came into my room and jumped on me sometime around 10 in the morning. I will never forget his face or his words when he said to me, "Rami, get up, we're under attack….and I'm *not* kidding you. Get up, something has happened." My first thought was, "He's got to be kidding me."

After all, this was Washington, D.C., not Beirut. I had grown up listening to stories of my family and relatives in the war-torn Middle East, but these stories were all a part of a distant place. I had no connection to this past my relatives spoke of, where so much went wrong and so many were killed…

There is no doubt that September 11 was a remarkable day for all the people of the world. For the people of this country, though, it was a turning point. No longer were we invincible. That vast ocean that separated us from the conflicts of the old world now seemed like a small stream.

The events of September 11 have changed everything for me. I am an American, born and raised in Chicago. I am also an Arab-American, with family in all parts of the Middle East. It is hard to explain to others how hard September 11 was for me. I had to stand by on that day and watch some men, all Arab, destroy buildings and lives in this country.

My life has forever changed. Every day, I have to watch people on television lash out and tear apart my culture, my ancestral lands, and my religion. I know in my heart that I did nothing wrong. Some part of me, though, feels responsible.

I have a new mission now…I must bring together two cultures, some may even say two worlds. In my heart, I know that Arabs and Muslims are good, hard-working people who desire many of the same things we do here in this country. There are certainly some zealots, but there are extremists in every culture and every religion. My new role as an Arab-American is to ensure that we do not embark on another Crusade. The important thing now for this world is communication and dialogue. By feeding into the myths of a "clash of civilizations" and a split between Islam and the West, we are helping to fuel the fire.

Reuben, age 18
Los Angeles
New York University

On September 11, I was awakened by surprised shrieks from outside as a commercial airliner plowed into one of the two towers that loomed large and indestructible just over a mile south of my dorm. Though I had only been in the city for a few weeks, I already recognized the World Trade Center as a symbol of the strength and perseverance of New York's citizens. New Yorkers had responded bravely a few years ago when a bomb exploded in one of the towers, and I knew that they would react just as boldly in repairing the damage done by the plane that (I assumed) had accidentally found its way into the side of the Trade Center building that morning. I stood leaning out my window, my eyes glued to the gaping hole in the side of the north tower as airplane fuel melted steel that provided its support. A few minutes later, I saw an orange explosion rip through the other tower as a second plane reached its final destination. Thousands of sheets of paper fluttered to the ground as larger unrecognizable items plunged more quickly to the pavement below. I am thankful that, at the time, I was unaware that some of these mysterious falling objects were people leaping from the flames engulfing their offices only to meet an equally horrible fate. By this time, the sidewalk below me was crowded with onlookers, some staring, as I was, in wide-eyed disbelief, others crying hysterically. The howl of sirens drowned out their sobs as ambulances, fire trucks, and police squad cars raced down the street. When the first tower collapsed, I was unsure what was happening. It seemed from my vantage point that something had combusted in the building sending a plume of gray smoke and ash into the air, adding to the dark cloud that had already blacked out the once blue sky over lower Manhattan. The second tower soon followed, and I felt sick to my stomach. There I stood, still staring out the window, unable to move or to do anything to stop the buildings from crushing the thousands of employees and firemen trapped inside. A sense of helplessness swept over me, and I finally left the window and turned on the television, where I learned of the two airliners that crashed in Washington and in Pennsylvania. I sat in front of the television for the rest of that day, terrified to leave my dorm. I did not fear for my life; I was afraid that if I left the TV unattended for even a few minutes, I would allow terrorists to strike again. The next time I looked at a clock, it was late in the day. I tried to call my mother in Los Angeles, but the phone lines were down and the call would not go through. The streets were dead silent that night, as roads were closed to allow for the passage of emergency vehicles making their way down to the site. Though the night was far more tranquil than any since I had arrived in the city, I did not sleep. I laid in bed staring at the ceiling, replaying the sights and sounds of the day in my mind. I imagined firefighters racing up the stairs directing employees to the nearest exit as the building rumbled and began to crumble around them. I thought of the fathers, mothers, siblings, children who would not be coming home that night, whose bodies would never be found under the countless tons of rubble constituting what were once called the Twin Towers. And like so many others around the world that night, I cried.

Annie, age 20
New York City, NY
Columbia University

…it hit me how surreal and unique our experience at Columbia was that day. We were in New York but at the same time we were uptown, over a hundred blocks away from the madness. We were in the eye of the storm to the rest of the world, but we were miles away from the horror. Everything around Columbia appeared normal, but on TV disaster was striking my city downtown. I experienced the madness through CNN just like the rest of the world did. I had learned about the attacks and seen the mass incident unfold on TV just as my family saw the same thing [from overseas]…I realized that the experience of September 11 was shared nationwide and worldwide. The World Trade Center attacks happened to all of us. We all went through the same horror.

Marcelo, age 19
Buenos Aires
New York University

As I write this, it has been slightly over six months since the attacks on the World Trade Center. To be honest, I can't pinpoint exactly how those events will affect the rest of my life. There is undoubtedly a pre- and post-September 11 timeframe in my mind. Since then, I feel an increased sense of urgency in how I carry out my life. Something I might not have done before due to embarrassment or fear of failure is now done anyways, because simply being young doesn't mean we have our whole life ahead of us. Additionally, my first instinct that day was to send out a mass e-mail telling everyone not only that I was not hurt, but also how much I appreciated and loved them.

However, I think these are short-term effects of the disaster. I don't think I have acquired the capacity to look back in retrospect and fully be able to extract the changes this has brought upon me. Perhaps there are some others see in me that I am blind to. But most importantly, what September 11 most left me with was the notion that September 11, 2001 does not mean the same thing to everyone. Neither does the United States flag. To me, the US flag signifies unity, tolerance, and possibilities, but others used that flag to preach xenophobic and igno-rant messages. Furthermore, all of us have been affected by September 11 whether we like it or not. The United States is at war, and we have fallen prey to that. September 11 has increased my socio-political vision, and has taught me more than ever to analyze, dissect, and deconstruct the current political climate.

Chapter 2:

A Generation Responds

"At Michigan and campuses all around the country, the generation that once had it all–peace, prosperity, even the dot-com dream of retiring at 30–faces its defining moment."[vii] "After the deadliest attack on American soil in the history of the republic, the generation that previously seemed directionless and without a fitting title now had one–*Generation 9/11*."[viii] So the story goes: A once-insular, once-apathetic generation has been forever transformed by catastrophe. America's young have been awakened from the consumerist slumber of the 1990s to face a redefined world. Overnight we have been reshaped into "Generation 9/11," ready to take up the mantle of leadership and face our nation's destiny. It's a familiar tale, perhaps because of its accessibility, perhaps because of the ease with which it is told, perhaps because of a national audience attuned to its positive message. But this tale is as manipulative as it is inviting. It avails itself of our country's need for patriotic optimism in a time of trouble rather than confronting the less comfortable reality: 9/11 is *not* a defining moment for this generation of young people.

September 11's significance for our generation is more complicated. On the one hand, it has provided young people with a newfound awareness of political issues, an awareness that does have the *potential* to transform us into an active and engaged citizenry. On the other hand, this awareness is both limited and fleeting. The emotional impact of September 11 has been channeled into a new interest in domestic and international policy issues related to terrorism and homeland security. But our awareness of these issues represents only a narrow understanding of politics, not a fundamental transformation of our attitudes or our actions. After September 11, less than one in ten said terrorism made them consider changing careers.[ix] Unless the limited awareness spawned by 9/11 is transferred into true political engagement, "Generation 9/11" will look more and more like it did on 9/10.

This chapter begins by assessing some of the proposed definitions of our generation. It outlines one of the most notable characteristics of today's youth: a demonstrated commitment to community service and a simultaneous negligence of political service. This dichotomy is understood as rooted in a rift between the purpose of government and a political process that is perceived as unsavory. In order to heal this divide, America's youth first need a broader, more sustained awareness about the possibilities of government, and second propulsion into the political process itself.

Defining a Generation

But before we can embark on an exploration of the effects of 9/11 on our generation, we need to reevaluate how this "generation" has been understood. Over the course of the 1990s journalists and pundits proposed a number of labels in an attempt to encompass and "define" young people, each of which followed the same path from sporadic acceptance to unanimous dismissal. The most popular and most notorious of these labels, "Generation Y," is a representative failure that misconstrues us as a mere extension of the generation before us. In 1991, novelist Douglas Coupland coined the term "Generation X," which reflected the feelings of apathy and cynicism widespread amongst twentysomethings at the beginning of the decade. The idea of "Generation Y" unfairly extends these characteristics to our generation, assuming that we have inherited the GenX sense of disenchantment. Another similar term, "Echo Boomers," again fails to define or understand us based on our inherent qualities by placing us in relation to our parents' generation, the Baby Boomers.

Other labels from the 1990s similarly fail to encapsulate our generation. Terms such as the "eGeneration" and the "MTV Generation" attempt to unite us based on features of contemporary American culture.

But these features are wholly exogenous to young America; they are features of our society over which we have no control. MTV is run by Generation X, and has become a corporate phenomenon that speaks *at* our generation without giving us any true voice. The Internet is a technological phenomenon that we have helped foster, but did not create and certainly cannot all access. These features fail to truly characterize our collective generational psyche. By artificially uniting us through superficial cultural phenomena, "eGeneration," "Net Generation," and other such labels avoid an exploration of our generation's inherent traits.

"Generation 9/11," a term recently coined by *Newsweek*, suffers from the same definitional problems. September 11 was a crucial moment in international relations, but one both caused and dealt with by our elders. September 11 has affected our generation in the same way it has affected the rest of the nation, but it was not an event generated by or for us, and hence cannot serve as a statement of our purpose. The Vietnam War was fought and supported, resisted and protested by young people; they were definitively shaped by the event because they were directly involved in its progress. Similarly, World War II shaped the Greatest Generation. Thus far, the War on Terrorism has not engaged our generation; we are neither decision-makers nor participants. As such, 9/11 does not constitute the defining moment for our generation; it, like MTV, is outside of our control.

The various attempts by our elders to categorize and define young America aptly demonstrate the futility of constructing an identity for our generation based on other generations or exogenous events. So far we have lacked any common experience through which we could unite, through which we could finally engage in the process of self-definition. In order to begin formulating an understanding of who we are, then, we must turn to our patterns of activity—what we have *done*.

A survey conducted by Harvard University's Institute of Politics in 2000 has shown that levels of engagement in community service are extraordinarily high among young people. In 2000, 60% of college students were involved in community service, a figure that testifies to our generation's passionate, idealistic tendencies.* The common perception that our generation is "apathetic" clearly does not stem from an overall assessment of our commitment to service. It seems derived instead from our contrastingly dismal commitment to politics: 64% of students do not trust the federal government "to do the right thing most of the time." Only 7% of young people have ever volunteered in a political campaign. Finally, 85% of young people feel that community volunteerism is better than political engagement for addressing issues facing the community. In order to understand our disengagement from politics, we must begin with one of its most important effects: our lack of a defined political agenda.

Young people have not identified which issues matter most to them as a constituency. We seem united more on lines of background, party, class, and ethnicity than we do on lines of age. This lack of a cohesive agenda has traditionally flustered politicians and prompted them to either one of two responses. The most common response among elected officials is to ignore our generation entirely. Because they do not see a "youth agenda," they do not know how to target us. Our dismally low voter turnout rates seem to confirm the idea that we are better off left alone. Without knowledge of which issues matter to us and without a sense that their time and money will result in votes, politicians reasonably opt to ignore us altogether. A second, occasionally popular strategy among elected officials has been the "youth gimmick." A politician who decides to target our generation cannot do so based on issues because he does not know what issues we care about. Instead, he uses charisma, attitude, and personality to strike a chord

---

* All quantitative data that is not cited comes from "Campus Attitudes towards Politics and Public Service," Harvard University Institute of Politics, October 2001.

with young voters, in the hopes that they will identify with him and that this identification will translate into votes. Bill Clinton's saxophone performance on "The Arsenio Hall Show" and his appearance on MTV ("boxers not briefs") embody this strategy. Governor Jesse Ventura, who touted his comic-book persona as a wrestler, and 2000 Presidential candidate Ralph Nader, who championed his connection with rock band Pearl Jam, are also prime examples of empty pandering to the youth vote.

Both of these strategies ultimately alienate our generation further from the political process, and confirm our suspicion of politicians, who we see as more concerned with votes than issues. As a result, we turn further away from the political process–which reinforces politicians' sentiments that targeting young people is a lost cause. Politicians and young people seem trapped in a vicious cycle that continually depresses our rates of involvement and our interest in politics. Before 9/11 over 50% of young people believed that political involvement "rarely has any immediate, tangible results,"[x] aptly highlighting our extreme dissociation from the political process. The goal of this book will be to examine just how important September 11 has been in reversing this dissociation and breaking the distressing pattern of neglect and disenchantment. But before we can do that we must ask why this dissociation came to exist in the first place, and why it has remained so pressing a problem.

False Oppositions

Our alienation from the political process is the result of two dichotomies. First, we perceive a split between the ideas of *government* and *service*. Young people have shown themselves overwhelmingly committed to localized, hands-on projects in their communities, such as working at shelters, volunteering in soup kitchens, and tutoring underprivileged children. These types of engaged activities are viewed as "service" in a pure sense. Results are tangible, immediate, and unequivocally positive, and participants make a direct impact on issues they care about. But where gratification from community service is high, gratification from government work seems unforgivably low. Over 85% of young people feel that community service is easier to take part in than politics. Young people also believe that community service is more effective for solving problems and is more enjoyable than government work. The political process seems indirect, imprecise, and slow—the antithesis of what we perceive as truly constituting "service."

To explain why we perceive government and service as such irreconcilables we must turn to a second dichotomy, the rift between the *purpose of government* and the *culture of politics*. Contemporary government has always had one purpose—to help the people. As defined in the Preamble to the U.S. Constitution, government exists to "establish justice, insure domestic tranquility, provide for the common defense, [and] promote the general welfare." The purpose of government is to serve the people; through its programs, legislation, and decisions, it seeks to provide citizens with a society in which they can flourish. Government has been and remains the primary way to make long-lasting, sweeping change, in the community, the nation, or the world.

Yet even while most Americans abstractly recognize the stated purposes of government, few see today's government as fulfilling those ideals and objectives. Young people especially fail to perceive government as an institutional framework for facilitating positive change—their experience is with a distasteful *political culture*, not ideals. First, politicians are seen as acting out of self-interest rather than for the general welfare or good of the country. In 2000, 74% of college students agreed, "elected officials seem to be motivated by selfish reasons." The representative politician to most young people is a fast-talking, hand-shaking, baby-kissing creature of ambition—someone whose glibness far exceeds his virtue. Second, politics is seen as unnecessarily bureaucratic and, as a result, hopelessly slow, impersonal, and indirect. Many young people see government administration as tied up in red tape, and unable to affect change that is felt by the people. Almost 60% consider government "the" government, rather than "our" government.[xi] Third, politicians are seen as slaves to campaign contributors. According to a youth poll conducted before September 11, "64% think that government is run by a few big interests looking out only for themselves."[xii] All of these contemporary perceptions of political culture can be reduced to the basic belief that politics is a dirty business that cannot and does not serve people.

Contemporary political culture in America was fashioned during the Second World War, when modern forms of mass communication were established and the government experienced a dramatic increase in bureaucratization. First, television and radio allowed politicians to reach the American public more effectively, permanently changing the nature of campaigns. Candidates could now promote themselves and their messages through advertisements, televised debates, and (in the case of 1996 presidential candidate Ross Perot) even infomercials–in addition to the usual round of stump speeches and whistle-stop tours. While the nature of democracy forces candidates to sell themselves to the public, modern forms of communication intensified this element of self-promotion. Politicians' public personas became both transmissible and reproducible and as a result were subject to a heightened amount of public scrutiny. It therefore became essential for politicians' television identities to be as impeccable and composed as possible; it meant developing a unique look and feel as a candidate–a personality. The presence of any one candidate on television forces all other candidates to follow suit, each striving to maintain his credibility and competitiveness.

A second factor in the development of modern political culture was the increase in government bureaucracy that emerged during the Presidency of Franklin Delano Roosevelt. Roosevelt's "New Deal" responded to the Great Depression of the 1930s in part by creating many new federal programs and agencies; the White House staff itself grew from 33 mostly clerical workers during the Hoover administration to 250 in 1953. Today the number is closer to 2,000 when one includes administrative units like the Office of Management and Budget, and the Council of Economic Advisors.[xiii] In the last half of the twentieth century these moves toward bureaucratization were codified and institutionalized. Today American government is more subdivided, compartmentalized, and complex than at any period in its history: in addition to the fourteen Cabinet departments, the Executive Office of the President consists of fifteen agencies and offices–a far cry from George Washington's four "advisors" in 1789. The natural result of this development has been the growing perception that government is slow and complicated, and that paper-pushing is the main task of government officials.

The twin forces of bureaucratization and mass communication have created a culture of politics that justifiably appears to our generation to be both inefficient and self-aggrandizing. Yet the rift between the culture of politics and the purpose of government would not be self-sustaining was it not for the powerful intervening force of the American media. While to an extent each of the above perceptions about politics are true, the media tends to disproportionately focus its coverage on these aspects of political life, often consciously ignoring hard news and generally downplaying the positive gains made by government. Almost all television channels, whether basic or cable, are owned by a handful of corporations, whose primary concern is profit. The American public has taught these businesses the unfortunate lesson that scandal sells–a lesson perhaps over-internalized by the media in the 1990s. OJ Simpson, Monica Lewinsky, and Gary Condit were arguably the three biggest news stories of the last decade; these episodic, intrigue-ridden stories promised more sustained high profits than the atrocities in Rwanda, relations with China, or education reform. Thin coverage of important issues veils the true purpose of government by reinforcing our negative impressions of the culture of politics.

Our generation has not experienced government as it can, should, and does exist. We face instead a version of politics that is bureaucratic, disengaged, and distasteful–a negative political culture part reality and part fantasy, part historical truth and part media-driven illusion. Our negative perceptions of "politics" have crystallized into a widespread generational belief that government cannot solve problems and that government work is not true service. Our definition of service has grown to exclude government work entirely and instead refers to local community action, an alternative we perceive to be more direct, more helpful, more engaging, and more gratifying.

While our generation's initiative and resolve in community service work is to be lauded, our inability to shed our fundamentally skewed image of government is both lamentable and dangerous. It is lamentable because it bars us from our country's most effective and fundamental tool of change and perpetuates a cycle of negligence between youth and America's leaders. It is dangerous because it sustains our perceived gap between government and service, a gap that may compromise the long-term vitality of our democratic state. If those of us who decide to serve in government are not serving the higher ideal of service, then we are slaves to the culture of politics. And if those of us outside government sustain this dichotomy, we will remain too disenchanted to care.

Bridging the Gap

Uniting the ideas of government and service in the minds of young people requires two distinct elements, *awareness* and *action*, which together create *engagement*.

Awareness: First, our generation must recognize that government can and does have an impact on society, whether for better or for worse. We must believe that governmental action is relevant to the lives of ordinary individuals. Awareness means understanding the proactive role that government plays in modern society and believing that government, like public service, can provide a vehicle for the creation of a better society. The second aspect of awareness is a desire to educate oneself about the salient political issues of the day. This requires the basic understanding that American society does not exist in a vacuum and that international political issues are relevant to everyday life. In short, awareness is a desire for a more thorough understanding of issues based on the recognition of the purpose, spirit, and influence of government.

Action: The second stage required to unite government and public service is *action*. Action can occur through voting, calling/writing one's representatives, discussing and debating issues, protesting policies, or signing petitions. Action may include writing letters to the editor, volunteering for campaigns, or serving in either an elective or appointive role in the government. Action is participation. Participation in the democratic and legislative processes works towards the creation of actual substantive policies, thereby translating the possibilities of government into realities.

Engagement: Awareness and action are each necessary elements for the mobilization of our generation into the political sphere. But neither by itself is sufficient to bridge the gap between government and public service. Awareness without action is powerless to influence or determine world affairs. Action without awareness neglects the purpose and spirit of government in favor of the culture of politics. Those who are perennially active run the risk of becoming disconnected from service, the real foundation of politics. A sustained combination of awareness and action is needed–*engagement*. Engagement is action that grows from a desire to serve, rather than from a desire for power or fame, or from the enjoyment of politics itself. Engagement is living the axiom that politics is a means to an end, not an end in itself.

These three stages towards uniting government and service are not easily realized, and as a result, efforts to bridge the gap have come up against four major stumbling-blocks. First, the general discussion of youth disengagement has suffered from an improper understanding of our generation. Instead of the paradigm of "Y," we must pursue processes of self-definition and agenda-formation, while recognizing these processes as crucial factors in overcoming our disengagement. Second, neither our generation nor our elders have identified the root causes of our dissociation. To the extent that the problem of youth political disinterest has been identified, it has not been linked to *both* of the dichotomies outlined above. While many have recognized the rift between government and service, its foundation in the dichotomy between the purpose of government and the culture of politics has been left sorely underdeveloped. Third, no policies have been implemented to address youth disconnect from politics. The fact that our generation is disconnected makes it unlikely that we will increase our civic engagement without some help from our elders–but adult policymakers have turned away with frustration from what they see as a disinterested, non-voting youth constituency. Finally, the unappealing culture of politics actively turns us away from government and towards community service. As long as political culture sustains our beliefs that government is corrupt, bureaucratic, and self-interested, we will remain disengaged from meaningful political action.

A Ray of Hope

Only extraordinary events can provide the impetus for changing paradigms about politics. These events provide a unique opportunity to create engaged citizens, but are unlikely to happen more than once in a generation. For all the tragedy and terror that the date still evokes, September 11 has acted as a ray of hope for our generation, by allowing us to take unprecedented steps towards ending our dissociation from the political process. 9/11 has bestowed on our generation a new sense of awareness; we are distinctly more cognizant of national security and military issues and our awareness of international politics has increased on a basic level. Yet the importance of this awareness seems relatively marginal. One year later, we still know little about the Social Security policies that will determine our future retirement plans. We still have little to say about the education reform proposals that will shape our children's' futures. We still recklessly ignore the increasingly dramatic energy crisis that could dramatically reshape our consumption patterns as adults.

And yet this basic, limited awareness *is* a crucial result of September 11; it is the first step to creating action and engagement. This importance is underscored by the patterns of political action among young people in the wake of 9/11. From the fall of 2000 to the fall of 2001, involvement in political organizations surged dramatically, from 16% to 28%.[xiv] However, while this change is impressive, it has only been effective in the short-term—by the fall of 2002 this number had dropped to 14%. For our generation to truly overcome its dissociation from politics, we will need to experience a general, sustained rise in *all* forms of political action. Political action is stymied by our anathema to the culture of politics, and it is only awareness that can break this vicious pattern.

Unfortunately, awareness is fleeting. Major events in American history have also prompted spikes in awareness, but, as Professor Robert Putnam notes,

> There is a well-understood half-life, and those spikes disappear…After an earthquake, it's gone after six months. After a snowstorm, its gone after something like three weeks…And after Oklahoma City, it lasted longer but…18 months after the bombing, the sentiment of connectedness was gone. There is only one example that I know of in recent American history in which the spike after a large calamity did not disappear very quickly—and that's Pearl Harbor.[xv]

But the motivating question of this book is whether September 11's effects on youth engagement will look more like those of Pearl Harbor or those of the Gulf War. During the latter conflict, the country experienced a surge in engagement unparalleled since the Vietnam War, but this new civic interest plummeted with the resolution of the war.[xvi] Even despite its inauguration with an important post-Cold War conflict, the 1990s were a decade of unprecedented apathy.

Preventing post-9/11 levels of awareness from declining is the problem that faces us today. One year later, we are still interested in government and we are still aware of the possibilities that government offers. However, our generation is struggling to translate this awareness into action and engagement. The 2002 midterm elections almost signified a return to normalcy–candidates continued to run personality campaigns on television and the media continued to search for scandal rather than address policy. Already the culture of politics is closing in on our gained awareness, undermining our new understanding of government. Time is running out.

The voices of our generation presented throughout this book are aware and impassioned, provoked and curious, but also frustrated. 9/11 has aroused in us a new understanding of the importance of government, an understanding as unexpected as the event itself. Yet unless we can convert this awareness into engagement–into conscious, purposeful action–we run the risk of forgetting everything that we have learned. 9/11 may very well be the rare event that allows us to finally cohere as a generation. But without civic engagement our agenda cannot be set, and generational self-definition will remain unattainable.

Alex, age 20
Los Angeles, CA
Stanford University

Every so often I escape from the university bubble to actually interact with the world, usually when I go back to the sleepier locale of North Carolina to visit my relatives. Even when I don't, however, I still try to pay attention to how people outside my bubble are behaving and understand on at least some level where they're coming from. To some campus leftists, the American people–that abstract and therefore almost totally amorphous conception–are an apathetic mass, either too stupid to care or, on charitable days, too ignorant and oppressed to join together in activist solidarity. But as far as I know, ordinary people are simply ordinary people, for the most part just concerned with doing a good job with their own lives and managing the problems and responsibilities that weigh on them. This, for most, is a full time job.

Every so often this complacency is impacted by something new or unexpected–not shattered, just impacted. September 11 may very well turn out to be a watershed moment in U.S. foreign policy, but if so it will not be on the strength of that one event alone–not any more than the Cold War was caused just by the Berlin Blockade. Change comes not just from events, but from the references and memories that stem from them–from the speeches, the books, the memorial services, and the tributes. The event only sets us on a certain course. Jesus was on earth but a few decades, but Peter was the rock of two millennia.

Those who lost loved ones have lost fellow-travelers in life, and of course their lives were changed. But have all our lives radically changed? Not as far as I know. We do the same things, we like the same drinks, we probably hang around with the same people, and we–for the most part–likely think the same sorts of thoughts. After all, those who hate globalization blamed globalization for the attacks–hence the WTO-cum-anti-war protests. Those who dislike immigrants haven't changed much either–only now they have an excuse. Even those of us who tend to humanitarian intervention now have a new excuse to push our angle, only now with a more politically palatable rationale. In general, I doubt very many people actually had their minds, opinions, or outlooks profoundly changed in the wake of those terrorist attacks. On the other hand–and here I think is the important part–a great many people did receive a violent and chilling reminder of what they already felt and knew. They were, if not converted, at least reawakened.

Americans remembered how proud they were to be American. Can we even guess at how many doctors, lawyers, businessmen, housewives, political moderates, students, university professors, journalists, and "ordinary people," with no particular political or polemical axe to grind, hauled out and raised up their flag? We remembered that the whole world was not like us, that our own little bubble was not impenetrable. We were reminded to appreciate a society that, whatever its flaws, keeps us safe and lets us live out our lives as we choose, in contrast to the majority of societies in the world.

We remembered how much New York really is American. For a time being, at least, New Yorkers were no longer the disgusting, debauched, and unforgivably immigrant, colored, or Catholic hordes whose revilers far antedate the Civil War. New York was once again a cultural capital, our door to the world, and a thriving metropolis of diversity, prosperity, and opportunity. In remembering that we were all New Yorkers, many of us were led to also recall how as New Yorkers we were, therefore, quintessentially American.

We were not the only ones who remembered. In Berlin, a crowd almost half a million strong took to the streets in support of the United States–they remembered that we were real people too, not just Yankees their leaders criticized, just as we once had that same realization as Soviet tanks and guns tried to seal off and imprison another vulnerable people. Our allies on the continent whose social elites are so wont to criticize us also remembered–only days after talks of an American-European split abounded in the press, the NATO countries unanimously came through and invoked the Article V collective-defense provision for the first time in history.

Enlightenment is a temporary thing. It is one thing to know, but quite another to understand. Almost all of us knew to appreciate all that we had: our friends and loved ones, our country, and our freedom. On September 11 and in the days thereafter, however, a great many of us actually dwelt upon this knowledge; we were relieved and thankful for those loved ones still with us. We felt struck by the stark manifestation of evil that reached out from the other side of the world to kill and, according to bin Laden, to crush us. We also came to realize how many people–real people–had already been killed and crushed by just that same evil.

The Enlightenment, I think, will not last. Most Americans have already gone back to their lives, to their own problems and issues and concerns. They may remember the experience of having the Enlightenment, and for the most part will live out their lives as before. Nonetheless, perhaps next time they have occasion to dwell a bit outside the bubble, and think on the innumerable tyrants, despots, and criminals whose authority extends over the sizable majority of humanity, their reaction will be less dismissive. Whatever happens, I only hope that, having been reminded for just one morning what the world is really like, we can all go about our lives with just a little more thanks and a little more concern for our fellow-man, whether he be across the seas or passing us on the street.

Julie, age 20
Portsmouth, RI
—

It's hard to say how things have changed in the university community since September. At the time, there was a huge outpouring of sorrow and sympathy, and people confessed their weaknesses to each other and committed to be better, more compassionate people. In general, though, people's behavior and attitudes remain unchanged from whatever they were before, because people still have the same weaknesses and strengths. If anything, people are slightly more tolerant and willing to accept people who don't fit in to popular culture.

It's difficult to describe the changes in the communities around me because public behavior has remained the same. Private behavior may have changed, and people may be storing more food and emergency supplies, but not where most people or I can see it. Maybe the only true recognizable change is that a strong divide has appeared between the nationalists and the skeptics; there is a suddenly a definable gap between those who support everything the U.S. has done and continue waving the flag for everything from shopping malls to McDonald's to the Olympics to our military campaigns, and those who point out that we were attacked because of the exploitative, manipulative nature of our economy and politics and believe that this attack on our so-called "Way of Life" means that we should change.

I work as a teaching assistant in a history of civilizations class that examines the issues of war and peace in a historical context, and this class has completely changed since I took it as a student a year ago. Because we focus on the problem of war, the fact that we have felt that threat personally makes our curriculum far more applicable than before. On September 11, we were one of the few classes that met as planned, and our discussion centered on our responsibility to "publish peace." In previous years, the class has had people very committed to promoting peace, but this year it seems that we are a little more savvy and critical of the actions of our government and even less disposed toward war. The students accept less at face value than they did before and are much quicker to ask whether there are alternatives to war.

Terrorism has not affected the way I live my life–I am never afraid for my personal safety because of it. However, my priorities have changed slightly, as reflected in how I spend my time. For example, I read a lot outside of class, and recently the scope of my reading has expanded to include economics, especially about globalization and the economics of communities. In my classes I am more interested in the repercussions on communities around the world from the global and international choices we make. Also, since I am planning to spend significant time abroad, I feel it is important to be able to protect myself. I started taking karate lessons at the beginning of this year because I know that there are plenty of anti-American activists all over the world.

I've recognized the Great Divide between politics and everything that's truly important. Christianity, Judaism, Islam, and Hinduism are essentially peace-promoting religions, yet they still produce terrorists bent on achieving political agendas. If my problem-solving strategy or method of passing judgment has changed at all, then, it has been through a new wariness of the hidden political agendas of others, and an increased ability to accept criticism. I've realized that humility and the ability to accept criticism is a necessary trait for politicians and good citizens in general, and it saddens me that the attacks seemed to make us even more proud. September 11 left me asking why the terrorists had attacked *us*. Though their attacks cannot be defended, I wonder whether they might have been somewhat justified in their opinions about the United States.

Shana, age 20,
Long Island, NY
Berklee School of Music

There's a lot of talk about the way in which such a vicious attack on American Soil has united our country, and how this camaraderie is the only way to "beat the terrorists." Everywhere I go now, I see slogans that are supposed to fuel patriotism. A local movie marquee reads, "We Love New York," while a bumper sticker warns that "United We Stand, Divided We Fall." The community has been brought together in a way that a genuine need for expanded recycling facilities or safer streets could never do. My notoriously unsafe neighborhood actually held a candlelight vigil, something that would have been considered something of a death wish before September 2001.

What frustrates me terribly is my inability to jump on the band-wagon. What I lack in patriotism I seem to have more than made up for in cynicism, and terrorism has led me to question everything. The concept of two passenger planes crashing into giant buildings ninety miles from my hometown is just so surreal that every conspiracy theory and every rumor seems as if it could be perfectly valid.

Unfortunately though, I'm smack dab in the middle of the wrong time to ask questions. I know that if I don't agree with my government's actions or policies, the vast majority of my starry-and stripy-eyed community is still following and supporting in blind faith. While the rest of my community is feeling genuine solidarity, I feel as if I'm totally ostracized. When a television commercial proclaims "God Bless America," I have to wonder where an atheist who doubts the integrity of our nation's leaders really fits in anymore.

I'm not holding a candle, and my favorite bumper sticker is the one that says, "Skateboarding is not a crime." On September 10 I was considered a rational, thoughtful student with socialist leanings. All of a sudden I'm Anti-American.

Terrorism has made people wary of sticking out from their community so much. It may not be fear alone that is breeding such strong solidarity, but fear certainly isn't hurting. My community seems huddled together so tightly that I wonder whether or not they can see the damage that they are doing to those that are left out. I don't want to be part of the huddle, and I don't want my own huddle. What I want is acknowledgement of a variety of opinions. If anything, I think that varied viewpoints can only make Americans stronger.

Scott, age 20
Marietta, GA
University of Georgia

The change in my community is not so apparent in the mannerisms of the citizens as it is in the masts of the flagpoles. I attend the University of Georgia, which is roughly 60 miles East of Atlanta. To say that the school is conservative is a severe understatement; while the rest of the nation views the native Stars and Bars as an insult, Georgians consider the flag a part of the Southern heritage. Amazingly, though, the dividing flags of Southern lore have been replaced with the unifying American Flag. The greatest change in our community is the actual community that can be seen after the cowardly acts of September 11. Infamous as a segregated society, our community has transformed into a society of Americans, rather than the compilation of different races that we were before the attacks. We, as Americans, have rallied around our liberties in this nation and the pride we have in saluting the true flag.

Terrorism was once an abstract concept for the majority of America, affecting only those who voyaged into uncharted or obviously unsafe areas. After the attacks on innocent Americans performing everyday duties, to say that each citizen did not feel a gasp of uncertainty would be a fabrication. As an individual, I must continue with my everyday life, because to live in fear would be to sacrifice my inalienable rights. Unfortunately, the attacks have altered my view of a race of people: I will never again be able to sit in an airport lobby without looking over my shoulder for militant Muslims eager to kill me in the name of a Holy War. Although this is a sad revelation, I know that I do not stand alone.

Colin, age 20,
Medford, NY
Bryant College

Young people like me sometimes take for granted the freedoms and opportunities that living in a democracy afford us. We've grown up to believe that the country we know and love as the United States is a powerhouse on both an economic and military front. September 11 served as a troubling reminder to my peers and me that no country and no person is free from the grasps of evil. There is no question that September 11 had tremendous ramifications on my everyday environment. At a small private institution like Bryant College, a tragedy that affects one is a tragedy that affects all. The loss of some peers and college alumni who perished in the terrorist attacks really compounded the pain and shock that many of us have felt.

The days and weeks after September 11 brought a tranquil spirit to my campus. As with the smaller-scale tragedies before this, we're often told to appreciate life, to ensure that each day counts, and so on. And, as before, the intensity with which we reflect on our good fortune gradually dissipates. But I think the attacks on New York City and the Pentagon are still affecting my college campus. There is no question that our commitments to celebrating the lives we have lost, and standing up for our flag, our country, and our democracy, are significant means by which we can unite and grow despite a catastrophe of this magnitude. This is true even despite the decreasing degree to which we grieve for human life and embrace our national pride.

The acts of terrorism will have a lasting effect on the people of this country...and they should. Talk shows and panel discussions are consumed with shedding some positive light or learning some artificial lesson from the inexcusable attacks of September 11. I think, however, that the two beams of light at Ground Zero that served as a temporary memorial until mid-April should be a long-lasting reminder of how short life is and how evil the world can be.

I am of the opinion that if the overall function of military actions is to eliminate terrorism, then we are somewhat misguided. The President, Secretary Powell, Dr. Rice, and Secretary Rumsfeld have all done a phenomenal job in reassuring Americans about the future and making terrorism an international priority, not just an American one. However, has the plan by which we will eliminate terrorism been articulated to the American people? Military strikes are crucial as a means of retaliation and punishment. However, military actions aren't going to mend fences with the "axis of evil," as President Bush called it. It's going to take an international coalition to overthrow governments, and transform these people's political and personal ideologies. In some cases it unfortunately challenges the religious beliefs of some of the people in these regions, which makes the mission of ending terrorism more complex, and perhaps impossible.

I would like nothing more than to put an end to terrorism, which breeds senseless violence and political hatred. But I'm concerned that the pain and anger after 9/11 may overshadow our judgment on how to proceed. Yes, we must fight terrorism and denounce its presence in our world. But when? For how long? Which countries will fight with us until the very end? How many countries do we invade? How many countries are going to retaliate? How many countries will retaliate with nuclear weapons? The President wants to send troops into Iraq to defeat Saddam Hussein. After Iraq, what do we do next? Where do we go next? The causes for the war on terrorism are clear. The means by which we will fight and be victors in the war are certainly not. We must proceed with extreme caution. Moreover, the people of the United States need to know, in every detail, what level of commitment is involved in expanding this war. This cannot just be the United States' war. Other countries must expend their resources and offer their troops to ensure this mission's expectations are met: that the world can rest better knowing that the evils and powers of terrorism are eternally put to rest.

Anna, age 19
Orem, UT
—

As soon as the events of September 11 became known, the change on the university campus became palpable, almost overwhelming. All was silent as students and faculty walked about stunned, incapable of comprehension or expression. This continued for several days and extended past the campus throughout the entire city. However, behind this wall of silence was a feeling of solidarity such as I have never felt before. When you bought your American flag at Wal-Mart, you knew that the cashier understood your pain and your motives. When waiting at a red light, you felt like a close friend of the person in the red, white, and blue car waiting next to yours.

Though we have moved on in many areas of our lives, that feeling remains. It is not as palpable as it was at the beginning, but upon immediate mention of that infamous date, it returns almost as strongly as in the beginning. When I visit my hometown, I feel a new strength and sense of purpose, coupled with a new soberness, which was especially present during the holiday season (which never seemed like much of a holiday).

I have also noticed a new sense of awareness in my hometown, and a desire for understanding and information. Suddenly my grandparents are experts on the Middle East and my younger siblings are bandying about political terminology and Arabic names.

On both the campus and in my hometown there is a greater feeling of paranoia. Conspiracy theories are accepted much more easily than before; security measures are expected and criticized for not being strong enough. Present also is a defensiveness when criticized by other countries, especially those in Europe. In the past, we used to accept these criticisms and apologize for being boorish Americans. Now there is a greater sense of pride in our crudeness and a sort of they-wouldn't-exist-if-it-weren't-for-us attitude. The widespread indignation that the act itself was committed, and that others are not as sensitive as they should be, is perhaps best expressed in my 14-year-old sister's email signature: God damn the terrorists, God bless the USA. Though I have not felt these changes as much in my religious community, there are more prophecies of the Apocalypse and the Last Judgment.

Overall, I think that there is a greater fear present, which is coupled with a greater feeling of determination, solidarity, and pride.

This is still quite recent for us. We're still sensitive, and nothing has fully sunk in yet.

Rebecca, age 19
Powder Springs, GA
Brigham Young University

Before September 11, I always thought of my plans for the future as pretty much a sure thing. I plan to go on to graduate school and then do research after that. Now I don't see the future as so certain. I still have plans and goals, but there is always the thought in the back of my head that I might not get to lead the future I would like. I think about how things must have been during the two world wars and the despair that people must have felt as all of their dreams were taken away. I used to have a hard time understanding the feelings that brought about some of the literature from that time period, the way that the writers felt such a lack of purpose in life, such hopelessness. Now I realize how lucky I am that I have never experienced the rationing of food items or having people close to me drafted into war. I thought about all of my male friends and how they are all right at the age of 19. They would be some of the first to get drafted if a draft was set up. I thought of my boyfriend and what it would be like to send him off to fight. It seemed like something out of an old movie that you just don't see happening now. I started thinking of my plans to do disease research in a whole new way. Instead of thinking about which disease I thought was most interesting that I would like to try and find a cure for, I started thinking about which viruses would be most likely to be used as weapons and what research I could do to protect our society against them.

Stephanie, age 20
Terra Haute, IN
Brigham Young University

In the wake of the September 11 attacks, everything changed. Flags were sold out across the state that day. Even the flag factory ran out.

Radio stations cancelled their contests and donated the money to humanitarian funds. People across the community put out their flags and cut out newspaper clippings regarding firemen as heroes. All the churches held prayer sessions and the Red Cross started blood drives across the nation. All these things happened right after, but they haven't really lasted. There isn't a big difference in the community anymore. The flags are on the shelves again. Radio stations are having their contests, and the newspapers are going back in the trash and recycle bins. There are more flags out than before, but most are leftover from the first few days and aren't noticed as much. Some marquees still have their slogan of "God Bless," but they are fewer every day. There are no more extra prayer sessions, and there are still blood shortages. I do think there is a slightly heightened awareness though. Troops are remembered in prayers more often and so are the nation's leaders. It seems people are more aware of and concerned with world events, too. At school, we don't really talk about it a lot, but there are more letters to the editor in the paper that deal with world events and terrorism and even the state of the nation.

Chapter 3:

Insecurity

Not since the sacking of Washington, D.C. in 1814, when British soldiers burnt the Capitol and the White House, had the continental United States suffered an assault as devastating as September 11. Though often compared to September 11, the December 7, 1941 attack on Pearl Harbor primarily involved military targets; few civilians were targeted or killed. Though the world lived under the constant shadow of annihilation during the Cold War, America herself remained unassailed. One of the thousands of casualties that lay in the ruins of the crumbling twin towers, then, was this peculiarly American myth of security, of invulnerability. Two stark, undeniable facts were thrust upon the American people: first, that many throughout the world hated the United States enough to inflict massive damage upon it, and second, that some of them had the wherewithal to do so.

For our generation, the shock was especially great. While our parents experienced the tumult of the '60s and the threat of nuclear annihilation and our grandparents sacrificed themselves to actively shape the course of the Second World War, our generation passively ignored our civic responsibilities while consuming the products of a way-laid commercial culture. In one horrible day, our world shifted from the comfortably inconsequential to the deadly serious. For the first time, not only did politics appear meaningful to vast segments of American youth but also pertinent to our everyday lives. For many, the necessity of establishing the correct balance between freedom and security became imperative. Some students feared an overreaction to 9/11 that might strip away civil liberties; others, trusting the president and his administration, believed an expansion in federal powers of investigation was necessary to maintain the security of the American homeland. Specifically, young people worried about the treatment and profiling of international students, the potential attenuation of student visas, and the interrogation of young Arab-American men.

On October 8, 2001, President Bush issued an executive order creating the Office of Homeland Security, naming Tom Ridge, the former governor of Pennsylvania, its Director. Ridge's mandate was broad yet simple: "to effectively coordinate counter-terrorism activities throughout all levels of government."[xvii] To fulfill this goal, Ridge and his team faced numerous complex challenges, requiring levels of innovation and integration that most experts would have considered impossible even a few years before.

In the weeks and months following 9/11, the Office of Homeland Security worked closely with the Department of Justice and other federal offices, such as the Immigration and Naturalization Service, to better equip the nation to resist future terrorist attacks. In particular, Attorney General John Ashcroft lobbied heavily for the USA PATRIOT Act, which, among other things, granted federal agents new authority over surveillance and wire-tapping. Moreover, the act enabled the government to detain non-US citizens suspected of terrorist activities for extended periods. Though many civil libertarian activists were alarmed, the defenders of the bill not only maintained its constitutionality, but also argued its essentiality for the defense of the nation.

The passing of the USA PATRIOT Act seemed to confirm many young Americans' feelings of marginalization from society. The overwhelming outpouring of patriotic sentiment, often taking the form of robust calls for justice (or vengeance), swept campuses throughout the country. While activists organized gatherings and protests calling for peace and understanding, most garnered little support. Many who chose to openly criticize the USA PATRIOT Act were denounced as anti-American. They, in turn, opposed what seemed to be excessive censorship and the absence of substantive debate.

One of the greatest concerns was the renewed controversy over racial and ethnic profiling, the practice by which law-enforcement officers target certain groups for criminal investigation. When the FBI began to question over 5,000 predominantly young Middle Eastern men in November 2001, many Arab-American organizations suspiciously labeled it "a form of racial profiling,"[xviii] a term that negatively grouped the interrogations with earlier controversies ranging from the Rodney King beating to the killing of Amadou Diallo by police officers in early 2000. When reports surfaced that the FBI had requested personal information on students from over 200 colleges, young people felt an even greater stake in the government's response to the attacks. While some compared these requests to the 'Red Scare' of the 1950s, many colleges complied, citing that several 9/11 hijackers had entered the country on student visas. For its part, the Bush administration defended the law enforcement agencies, claiming that they had made conscious efforts to avoid any form of racial profiling. Moreover, a growing number of dissenting liberals have argued that racial profiling is acceptable in this particular case; the Gallup Organization even found that 71 percent of African-Americans, the traditional victims of racial profiling, supported racial profiling after September 11.[xix]

National immigration policy also came under fire. All of the hijackers had entered the country legally and had slipped and blended into U.S. society, even though some stayed past the expiration of their visas. This raised big questions about whether America's rather porous borders encouraged terrorist groups to establish themselves within the country and about whether the Immigration and Naturalization Service (INS) was acting effectively and efficiently. The flaws in the INS system became readily apparent on March 12, 2002, when a Florida flight school received approved student visas for two of the deceased hijackers, Mohammed Atta and Marwan Al-Shehhi. Although the INS said that the visas were lost in a "backlog" and thought that a new $34 million tracking service would stop such mistakes in the future, President Bush was less sanguine, describing himself as "plenty hot" when hearing of the error.[xx] In another embarrassing incident just four days later, four Pakistani crew-members of a Russian tanker were allowed to enter the country at Norfolk, Virginia on short-duration visa waivers. One of the men had previously been expelled from the United States, and on arrival, all four disappeared. While none of these four men have any known ties to any terrorist or extremist organizations, this case symbolized to many the culture of ingrained incompetence that seemed pervasive throughout the INS.[xxi]

At the same time, however, this final case symbolized the fears of many activists, young and old, concerning immigration policy: Why should these four Pakistani men be singled out? Are these the only people who have flouted immigration law? Are these men only receiving such heavy attention, and the INS suffering such heavy criticism about this case, because of irrational, xenophobic fears concerning Muslims and Muslim countries?

Additionally, others feared that the government might take advantage of this crisis to increase the power of the INS–perhaps making life miserable for all immigrants, legal and illegal, from all over the world. Indeed, these fears were not completely unwarranted: A security bill passed in the Senate on April 18, 2002 that strengthened the INS, increased the number of border marshals and inspectors, and allocated funds to the improvement of border security technology. At the same time, the bill mandated closer supervision of foreign student visas, establishing systems that keep track of foreign students and the institutions hosting them.[xxii]

This development affected the college-age generation directly and has generated a number of questions: Could these new laws be used to reduce the numbers of certain nationalities of students considered undesirable? Will they discourage and deter talented foreign students from applying to American schools? Not only would this be detrimental to such students, it would reduce the chances for American students to encounter different cultural perspectives. Discussion and criticism of the stricter student visa rules did occur on campuses: students demonstrated awareness of the nation's policies when those changes directly affected them. They recognized the importance of the debate to their lives and struggled to make their voices heard, whether or not policymakers were listening.

Preeti, age 24
Lexington, KY
University of Kentucky

In mid-November of 2001, my father made a trip to India to visit my 88-year-old grandfather. On previous occasions, while traveling alone as a single brown-skinned male, my father had been racially profiled at European airports. After the September 11 attacks, my family wondered what he would be subject to at U.S. airports.

My mother and I drove him to the local airport. We arrived extra early, not sure what he'd encounter. Increased security measures required that cars not be left unattended at the curb, so I waited in the car while my parents went inside. A security officer paced by the cars. "Is he eyeing me suspiciously because I'm brown, or is it a figment of my imagination?" I nervously wondered to myself. "Be on your 'best' behavior. Don't do anything that would seem out of the ordinary."

Forty-five minutes later, my mother returned. She was half-laughing. "They opened up his suitcase on a table in front of the check-in counter," she explained. A young college-aged woman wearing latex gloves had rummaged through the suitcase's contents. She unfolded his underwear and shook it out. The boxes of Bic pens intended as gifts for my not-so-wealthy relatives in India were opened. The pens were tested to see if they wrote. What made my mother laugh? It was all the gifts intended for female relatives. Here my father was, standing in an airport, with a suitcase containing an unusual amount of "girly" stuff such as hair bows, lace, and Avon cosmetics. Furthermore, the young woman was unable to cram all of my dad's stuff back in his suitcase afterwards, so my mother had to repack everything.

As my mother and I drove off, my mother concluded, "I guess I can't blame them."

Even I have to agree that racial profiling is permissible at a time like this. It's not being done out of pure prejudice. Face it: All the terrorists so far have been brown-skinned, "Arab looking" men. Racial profiling is an efficient and effective means of identifying people that are possible terrorists.

My only request is that it be done in a way that doesn't humiliate and degrade the individual. I'd be mortified if my undergarments were rummaged through in sight of everyone at an airport. I don't want everyone eying me and thinking, "That person might be a terrorist." Yes, search more carefully those people fitting the profile of a terrorist. But please, make it discrete and away from the crowd. We can devise creative ways of pulling aside certain-colored people without having to draw the attention of the crowd. No innocent person wants the crowd, through their suspicious stares, to be branding him or her a possible terrorist.

Regarding racial profiling and other restrictions of civil liberties, we must have a plan for when the restrictions will end. Possibly, have a review of the policies every four months and decide if any can be lightened. Determine what conditions must be met in order for restrictions to be lifted completely. Basically, have a plan specifying just when the restrictions will end. Otherwise, we will be living indefinitely with limited civil liberties and undermining the very values we seek to defend.

A few weeks ago, I was logging my computer onto the Internet. When the initial screen appeared, I saw the headline, "Pentagon Considers Planting Fake News Stories." Shocked, I read on about how some had proposed that the Pentagon be granted the power to plant false news stories in foreign media outlets such as Reuters. "This is outrageous," I thought, "A government that's about democracy and freedom can't do something like this!"

I realize that our federal government cannot tell the world everything. Certain activities must be kept secret for security reasons. But outright lying? If you can't tell the truth, say nothing at all! My distrust of the government has increased. Maybe the government is lying to all of us right now! Am I a paranoid freak?! Can I trust anything the government says? As citizens of a democratic republic, Americans are their government. Why do I now feel as if my government is "the other"?

One of my friends' father, who is originally from Iran, says that the biggest difference between Iran and the U.S. is that people in Iran want freedom and democracy while people in the U.S. have both, yet don't take full advantage of them. Now, more than ever, is a time for us to exercise and appreciate the liberties we do have, for it is at war-frenzied times such as this when they are most in jeopardy. In particular, we must cherish freedom of speech as guaranteed to us in the First Amendment of the U.S. Constitution. An event as horrific as the September 11 attacks challenges us to critique the accepted order and fundamentally reorient our foreign policy. We must listen to our leaders, but we must also listen to ourselves. I hear our leaders say, "You're either with us or against us." What a false dichotomy!

We must apply the critical thinking skills we acquired in our educations. Seriously question the accepted order. If you end up disagreeing with it, don't be afraid to jump off the bandwagon and swim against the current. Speak up; that's one of the paramount freedoms that we have.

Kristyn, age–
Atlanta, GA
Flight Attendant

When I heard about the attacks on September 11 I was boarding a flight to Orlando. I was called for this trip the morning of the 11th and was told to report at 8:30. (We always arrive one hour before departure.) When I got to the gate I was told that I would be the On Board Leader (OBL) for the flights I was working today. The OBL is in charge of making sure the flight runs smoothly. About 9:00am we began the boarding process. It was just like any other day. About 9:30 we were getting ready to shut the door and depart when the agent frantically told me to get everyone off NOW. She said American [airlines] had been hijacked. The first thing that went through my mind was that the plane was close to Atlanta and they were trying to talk them out of what it was. I made a P.A. to the passengers and asked them to deplane, but stay close to the gate, and more information would be given there. The passengers were very upset. One lady yelled at me about her non-refundable hotel at Disney World. As the passengers were getting off, the captain came up to me and said the Pentagon had been bombed. At this point we had no idea what was going on. We were instructed to inspect the plane when everyone got off, then report to the crew lounge. When we got to the lounge about thirty minutes later 200 other flight attendants were in front of the TV. I could not believe what I saw. We all sat there in disbelief. I was numb. Two hours later they told us all to go home and wait for further notice on when flights would resume. The whole way home I kept thinking more attacks were about to happen. By this time all of Delta's planes had been accounted for. My roommate (also a flight attendant) and I did not leave the TV for one minute that day. We were sad for the flight crews and the families and realized it so easily could have been one of our flights.

Since the attacks I have noticed a lot of changes in security. At first the lines were so long. They did very thorough checks of each individual. It took a while for the screeners to learn their new job. They were taking things that I had in my bag for years (tweezers, can openers, and bottle openers). Things the average person would never think of as a weapon. Shortly after, I worked an international flight, and all our silverware was gone. We were boarded plastic silverware. One passenger was very upset she had to eat with plastic. Sometimes we try to explain to passengers why, and they don't want to hear our excuses. Besides security, procedures on the plane have changed as well. Security has gotten better although it can still be a hassle. I have had to take my shoes, belt, and sweater off. They have opened my bag (which can be embarrassing) and taken everything out one-by-one. Sometimes I get annoyed, but now I know that it comes with the job. I can see how travelers would be bothered by this.

Before 9/11 we would just get on the plane, store our bag, and begin getting ready for the flight. We'd check our emergency equipment, put supplies away and do any last minute things and hang out. It was very relaxed and a lot of fun. Now, on the first flight out each day we need to do a galley sweep. This means we take everything out of their drawers and slots. We open garbage cans, ice buckets, meal carriers, and anything else that is in the galley. This can take up to ten minutes. Then we have to brief with the captain and decide on a code word. This is the word that is used to gain entrance into the cockpit. On every flight a different word is used. If you don't use that word during the flight the pilots will assume there is a terrorist on board and you are in distress. So this word is very important. Sometimes we have to check seat pockets, tray tables, and under the seats. This takes a long time when it's needed. We don't really have a lot of down time anymore. We also have to check every bag of supplies that is boarded. This would be the cans of drinks, napkins, etc. We also look in the overhead bins. During boarding the OBL is instructed to look at each person in the eyes and say hello. Although we cannot discriminate, we are to look for suspicious people. I personally have never seen one. We also can't leave the boarding door because someone could easily gain access to the ramp area. There is a door to the outside by each plane. If we don't catch someone that goes in that area we are fined by the FAA. The fines can be very hefty. The flight attendants have to be a lot more aware than they used to.

Today I went to pick my parents up at the airport, and had to go through security. There were a few things I noticed that would be very annoying to the everyday traveler. I had just bought a Coke before I went through security, and they made me dump the whole thing before proceeding. I said you have to be kidding, I just bought it. He definitely wasn't kidding. Usually we would have to take the lid off and take a sip. Today he wouldn't let me. I think there are a lot of inconsistencies among the different airports. They let me pick my parents up at the gate because I had an airline I.D. It was very easy for me to gain access to the gate area. The lines were relatively quick too. Up until a few months ago you could wait in line for two hours to be cleared through the gates. In that aspect security has gotten better. The gate agents do random security checks as well. They choose a person and will search their entire bag and give them the wand. I notice a lot of passengers get really upset about this. It delays the whole boarding process. I think people have to accept that this is our society today. Everyday when I'm at work I wish it could go back to pre-9/11.

I don't have too much to say about the way I approach my job. Immediately after 9/11 I was a little paranoid. My first flight back I went to D.C. We were the 4th plane to land at Dulles since the attacks. Our flight was just about empty and we took off several hours late. Every time I heard a strange noise I would jump a little. I was definitely on my highest alert. Before I left I called my parents and boyfriend to let them know where I was going. That was a little strange because I never do that. The rest of September was pretty much the same. I was aware of the passengers and what was going on the entire flight. I noticed that other passengers were the same. I recall some people telling me if anything happened I could count on them. Then they would tell me their seat numbers. I remember most passengers being very nice after the attacks. People used to get really upset if we had to check their bags, or if they didn't have a meal choice. After flying a few more times I began to feel very comfortable with the job. Now I just think of the new procedures as part of my job. I now feel confident that a terrorist attack of that nature will never happen again. It took a few months for the FAA to figure out what pilots are to do in the event it ever happens again. I am not really allowed to talk about the procedures, but I'm confident that they will work. I also know what weapons I can use as a flight attendant. We have the halon and H20 extinguisher, hot coffee, and other tools in the galley for protection. Our airline is offering self-defense classes this summer. I think I will learn a lot from that.

Casey, age 21
Elizabethtown, KY
University of Kentucky

The September 11 terrorist attacks pushed a number of issues to the forefront of the American consciousness that are typically not thought of as particularly important. Perhaps chief among these issues is the state of religious harmony in America. Relations between people with different religious beliefs are only rarely discussed in everyday dialogue, but September 11 caused a number of Americans to actively pursue knowledge about non-Christian religions. Considering how little the concerns and viewpoints of these other religions, particularly Islam, are represented in mainstream society, I find the sudden growth of understanding quite compelling. September 11 will always be remembered first and foremost as a tragedy on the grandest scale, but even in tragedy some issues of hope for the future have arisen. It is my desire that the average American will become more sensitive to those of different religious persuasion, helping to usher in a new era of tolerance in our society.

Overall, I would have to say that I am pleasantly surprised with the Bush administration's domestic security proposals after September 11. In the days following the attacks, I envisioned massive internment camps akin to those of World War II, and to the extent that the administration has thus far restrained itself from these types of measures I am relieved. Bush unequivocally denounced violence against Muslims living in America, and has appeared publicly opposed to racial or ethnic profiling in airport security checks. However, it is difficult to overlook the USA PATRIOT Act and the vastly expanded power it has given law enforcement and intelligence agencies to spy on American citizens. While I recognize that such proposals could have been far more draconian, this does not ameliorate the effects of the "Big Brother Bill." In essence, while I am heartened by President Bush's stances on religious violence and ethnic profiling, I see much greater long-term danger in the provisions of the USA PATRIOT Act. The only bright point I can find in the legislation is that it could have been much worse.

To a much greater extent than many of my civil libertarian colleagues, I recognize the vital role that intelligence services play in national security, and I feel that they should be granted some latitude in investigations. However, my position on this comes down to what may be a technicality: the Constitution does not apply outside U.S. borders. When it comes to increases in the ability of law enforcement and the intelligence community to conduct surveillance inside American borders, I see no need for increased authority. Many of the provisions of the USA PATRIOT Act eviscerate normal American ideals that individuals have a right to privacy, violable only on particularized suspicion based on probable cause, *with* a judicially issued warrant. However, perhaps most disturbing is that these supposed increases in security would have had no effect whatsoever had they been in place prior to September 11. As I see it, no manner of domestic spying, no matter how invasive, would have prevented the attacks. If we truly wish to detect and deter future terrorist attacks, the only option is to increase human intelligence assets inside of the terrorist organizations themselves. While this presents numerous issues of human rights abuses, I would vastly prefer to have an "unsavory character" feeding information to the CIA in order to prevent another tragedy, as opposed to the useless dragnet proposals of the USA PATRIOT Act.

To be blunt, calling the debate between protecting civil liberties and ensuring security a "balance" is a red herring. The Constitution is not a scale, with varying interests given different weight depending on the tide of popular opinion. It is an absolute wall to certain government actions, and the concept that civil liberties somehow deserve less protection during wartime is to me grotesque and inconceivable. America has existed, through periods of both prolonged war and prolonged peace, for well over 200 years, and the permanence of the Constitution has been a major reason for that. I view "suspensions" of constitutional rights in times of crisis as nothing more than calculated maneuvers for short-term political gain. It has been demonstrated time and again that security can be achieved without needlessly exposing innocent people to heavy-handed tactics, but those lessons of history have apparently been lost.

Kristina, age 22
Phoenix, AZ
University of Arizona

September 11 was an eye-opening experience for me not only because it was the first terrorist attack for which I was alive, but also because the aftermath of the tragedy, with regards to legislation and executive orders, is like nothing I have ever seen. I find the willingness of both the government and the public to trade civil liberties for security equally as alarming as I found the attack on America.

In order to protect Americans against terrorism, the USA PATRIOT Act dictates that terrorism shall be defined as activities "threatening to cause, or have as their aim to cause, injury to or adverse effect on the United States, its citizens, national security, foreign policy, or economy." What happened to our freedoms of speech and dissent? Couldn't this broad definition of terrorism label me, as an ACLU student activist, a terrorist for participating in war protests and criticizing the actions of my government?

What astounds and terrifies me most is that I hear very few of my fellow students and peers denouncing these threats to our civil liberties. I have been told more than once that I am an "un-American, terrorist supporter" because I criticize the President and doubt the validity of this so-called "war." I ask myself what could possibly be un-American about putting to use the liberties outlined in the Bill of Rights.

Is the true "American" response to rally blindly around the flag during this time of crisis? This type of blind faith has lead to many troubling results. Dissent is being quelled through legislation and society's refusal to think beyond the propaganda the government churns out. Minorities are being marginalized through racial profiling and suppression of unpopular political views. Privacy is being eroded through expanded surveillance, searches, and wiretaps. These results don't seem to reflect the notions of freedom on which our country was founded.

If we want to be secure and protect ourselves from another attack, perhaps the best thing we can do is work towards understanding the causes of September 11 and reevaluate the ways we deal with international conflict. Individuals should not be profiled based on race or religion, but rather, based on their actions. Terrorists do not all look the same or follow the same religious dogmas. Thus, the government should look to protect us by focusing efforts on suspicious behavior, such as learning to fly planes without wanting to know how to land or take off. Racially profiling those responsible for 9/11 would not have saved us, but perhaps questioning suspicious actions could have. Rather than restricting civil liberties, the government should investigate why our intelligence and law enforcement agencies failed to detect the attack before it occurred. I suspect this information would be more helpful than attempts to question more than 5,000 men based solely on the fact that they are of Middle Eastern descent.

A time of crisis does not mean that we need to choose between being secure or being free—we can be both! As the president of the student chapter of the ACLU at Arizona State University (ASUACLU), I ask my fellow activists to think about this question: what is the point of being safe if we don't have the freedom to exercise our civil liberties? We should not be so quick to assume that the best way to be secure is to give up our freedoms. The ASUACLU will continue to participate in war protests and put on public events aimed at educating the public about the gross civil liberties violations outlined in Bush's counter-terrorism proposals. We will monitor legislation locally and nationally and write to our legislators. We will continue to join progressive alliances and work toward keeping our country safe and free.

If other activists do the same, perhaps the Bush administration will reevaluate its actions and stop molesting the Bill of Rights.

Chapter 4:

Guns and Butter

Our analysis has thus far considered issues relating to September 11 that have generated immediate interest among young people. The intent of this book, however, is not merely to examine passively the ways people of this generation have reacted, but how they will respond. If we were to stop at the responses garnered thus far, we might very well miss those issues of international concern that might be most important to our generation in the future, issues which currently receive little, if any, attention among us. The mindset, attitude, and awareness of our generation must respond and change in the wake of September 11 on a broader scale than is currently fathomable. That, more than the outside factors that adversely affect our lives, is what will determine the progress of our nation in the first half of this century.

Shortly following the attacks on the World Trade Center and the Pentagon, every person in America could recite facts about the ongoing war on terrorism and its relation to events in the Middle East and Central Asia. America's youth were aware of the world outside America's borders and that American actions had both concrete effects on her neighbors near and far and repercussions for her own people. Yet there is a distinct superficiality to this awareness, which does not necessarily attest to any true understanding or comprehension of the importance of our international relationships.

The shocking events that unfolded in front of American youth had a real and significant initial impact, but with each day that passes, the sense of immediacy and relevance fades. When left to examine the impact September 11 had on the average young American, one often fails to uncover stirring results. Tightened domestic security, increased media coverage of highly specific international events–these kind of changes may cause us to pause and ponder our place in the world for a moment, but they certainly do not reflect definitive impact.

When compared to the immediate paradigm shifts caused for generations of youth growing up in the WWII or Vietnam eras, the events of September 11 on the surface appear to offer fewer reasons for young people to react with decisiveness or tenacity. Discussion of youth involvement in World War II conjures romanticized images of young men leaving for war with well-wishing young wives behind them. Vietnam sparks memories of riotous anti-war protests on college campuses throughout the nation. However, one is hard pressed to settle on such a picture of youth involvement in post-Cold War military action. While there are many examples of young people who are aware of the military and nation-building issues discussed below, as a generation we have yet to give them any serious consideration. This is the problem we seek to address in this chapter, first by outlining the major military interventions of the post-Cold War era and second by discussing youth perception and involvement in military and defense issues before and after September 11.

Background Information on Post-Cold War Military Actions

Following the breakup of the Soviet Union and the end of the Cold War, the relatively simple dynamic of a U.S./Soviet global standoff gave way to a complex new strategic situation. Although the U.S. was able to drastically curtail its defense expenditures, it had to restructure its force composition so that it could effectively fight multiple regional conflicts in problem areas such as the Middle East and the Korean peninsula. Without the threat of Soviet nuclear retaliation, the U.S. essentially had a free hand in global affairs and became involved in an unprecedented number of military missions including the Gulf War (1990-91), Somalia (1992-94), Yugoslavia (1992-94), Bosnia (1993-95), Haiti (1994-96), Croatia (1995), Sudan (1998), Afghanistan (1998), Kosovo (1999), Colombia (2000), and Macedonia (2001). The Gulf War,

Somalia, and Bosnia provide three representative examples of interventions that illustrate the main types and characteristics of U.S. policy.

On August 2, 1990, the Iraqi army invaded and occupied Kuwait. To justify the invasion, Saddam Hussein accused Kuwait of violating oil production limits set by the Organization of Petroleum Exporting Countries (OPEC). Iraq also claimed territorial rights to Kuwait. On August 6, the UN Security Council imposed an embargo prohibiting trade with Iraq except for food and medical supplies. The next day, the U.S. announced that it would send troops to the Persian Gulf to defend Saudi Arabia from possible attack. Several months later, economic sanctions had failed to force Iraq to withdraw from Kuwait. The U.S. supplied 425,000 troops to a UN coalition, which included 37 other countries. On January 17, 1991 air strikes signaled the beginning of what came to be known as *Operation Desert Storm*. Initially, aircraft targeted Baghdad, Iraq's capital. Then, heavy bombing was focused on Iraqi troops, artillery and tanks, transportation routes, ammunition supplies, and chemical/biological weapons facilities.

The ground war consisted mainly of one massive attack. On February 24, coalition forces simultaneously invaded Iraq and Kuwait from several different points. Troops quickly broke through Iraqi fortifications, and more than 60,000 Iraqi soldiers surrendered. On February 26, Hussein's army was surrounded and he ordered his troops to withdraw. The U.S. officially ended all operations on February 28–approximately 100 hours since the attacks started. Iraqi deaths, both military and civilian, were estimated at well over 100,000, while only 480 coalition troops were lost.

In many ways, the Persian Gulf War was the United States' most successful post-Cold War intervention. First, the U.S. had a clear and vital interest in the region's oil. Second, the public, Congress, and key allies strongly supported military action. Third, evicting the Iraqis from Kuwait was a well-defined, achievable objective. Finally, the American victory confirmed that the use of decisive amounts of firepower and troops would avoid the kind of incremental escalation that led to disaster in Vietnam. However, the Gulf War had one very important consequence–Osama Bin Laden, the leader of the al Qaeda terrorist network, objected to the presence of U.S. soldiers in Saudi Arabia. During the next decade, he embarked on a terrorist campaign against the U.S. that ultimately culminated in the September 11, 2001 attacks on the World Trade Center.

In 1993, civil war erupted in Somalia. Rival factions supported Mohammed Ali Mahda and Mohammed Farah Aidid. The fighting, coupled with the worst African drought and famine in a century, resulted in a horrific 300,000 deaths. 30,000 American troops had entered Somalia in December of 1992 as part of a UN mission named *Operation Provide Relief*. The UN brokered a peace between the rival warlords on January 15, 1993. However, after a June 29 ambush killed 24 Pakistani members of the UN peacekeeping team, President Clinton sent 400 Army Rangers to Somalia with orders to capture Aidid. The U.S. became actively embroiled in Somali politics and operations entered a second phase known as *Restore Hope*.

On October 3 and 4, Army Rangers were engaged in a fierce firefight when followers of Aidid surrounded them during a raid in Mogadishu, Somalia's capital. In what constituted the most severe combat losses for a single unit since Vietnam, 75 soldiers were wounded and 18 were killed. (The ill-fated raid later became the subject of the book and movie *Black Hawk Down*). In addition, graphic televised footage of a dead American soldier being dragged through the streets and images of a captured helicopter pilot turned U.S. public opinion against continued presence in Somalia. President Clinton ordered the Rangers out of the country, and on October 7 he pledged to withdraw all forces. However, extraction proved complicated, as Clinton first had to send more troops to provide support for the withdrawal. All involvement did not end until March 25, 1994 when the last contingent of 25,000 troops withdrew from Mogadishu.

Somalia was regarded as a public relations debacle. The mission had proved problematic for a number of reasons. First, by the time Clinton sent the rangers to capture Aidid, only about 3,000 U.S. troops remained in Somalia. Also, most of these were under UN command.

Second, there was no clear policy on how to deal with the warlords. Most importantly, media coverage undermined public support. In the aftermath, leaders were very skeptical about the future use of limited force for humanitarian interventions.

In March of 1992, Bosnian Serbs laid siege on the capital city of Sarajevo. By the end of spring, the Yugoslav National Army controlled 60% of Bosnia-Herzegovina. Many Muslim and Croatian citizens were massacred or sent to death camps as Bosnian Serbs conducted an ethnic cleansing campaign. Croatian forces retaliated by perpetrating atrocities against Serb civilians. After attempts to achieve a political settlement failed, NATO launched the largest military action in the alliance's history. In May of 1995, *Operation Deliberate Force* began. After two weeks of air strikes and a strong Muslim-Croat offensive on the ground, the Bosnian Serbs agreed to negotiate. The Dayton Peace Accords split Bosnia into the Muslim-Croat federation and a new Bosnian Serb republic. 60,000 international troops under NATO command entered Bosnia to serve as peacekeepers.

Bosnia seemed to reaffirm the belief that limited war could be effectively employed to achieve diplomatic goals. However, several concerns arose in the following years. The many countries composing the NATO force that continues to occupy Bosnia have found it difficult to sustain solidarity as typical disagreements about which forces should perform what roles have arisen. Remembering the situation in Somalia, the U.S. has kept most of its soldiers under direct U.S. command. In addition, the region continued to be troubled after the Dayton Peace Accords. In 1999, the Serbs began massacring ethnic Albanians in the province of Kosovo. NATO responded with *Operation Allied Force*, a massive 79-day air strike that eventually succeeded in curbing the aggressions of Serbian leader Slobodan Milosevic. This bombing campaign, in addition to the 1995 actions, has left the region utterly devastated. It will require billions of dollars to repair the damage and revive the Balkan economies. Many Serbs still greatly resent NATO's bombing of their country and are extremely hostile toward the U.S. and its allies.

Currently, the United States maintains around 10,000 troops in Bosnia. Critics have repeatedly questioned America's commitment, arguing that it is costly and diverts resources from more important regions. But soon after September 11, officials began re-evaluating the effectiveness of U.S. forces in Bosnia: A new, emerging consensus sees nation-building as complementary to America's efforts to fight terrorism. The capture of six Algerian al Qaeda members in Bosnia hammered home the point that war-torn regions are potential breeding grounds for terrorist activity. By diffusing tension in Bosnia through extensive relief efforts, the U.S. now hopes to prevent it from becoming a serious problem area.[xxiii]

In 1994, a group of young Islamic fundamentalists in Afghanistan united to form a powerful military group intent on taking control of the country. By 1996, the Taliban had two-thirds of the country in its grasp and had seized control of the capital city of Kabul. However, only three countries, Pakistan, Iran, and Iraq, were willing to recognize the legitimacy of this new national government. The UN supported the Northern Alliance, the main opposition to the Taliban, and acknowledged Burhanuddin Rabbani, originally selected as the interim president in 1992 before the coup, as the country's rightful leader.[xxiv] Strict, repressive governance characterized the rule imposed by the Taliban. From the destruction of ancient giant Buddhas carved into the mountainside to limitations on the dress and behavior of women, the Taliban earned the disgrace of the international community. In the years after the takeover, civil war between the Taliban and the Northern Alliance destabilized the country, even despite U.N. attempts to broker a peace agreement.

In 1998, the United States bombed terrorist camps in Sudan and Afghanistan in retaliation for attacks on U.S. embassies in Kenya and Tanzania. The U.S. also demanded that the Taliban turn over Osama bin Laden, the man responsible for the two attacks. When, in 1999, Taliban officials acknowledged that bin Laden was living in Afghanistan under their protection but refused to surrender him, the

U.S. froze Afghan assets in U.S. territory and banned trade with the Taliban.

Operations in Afghanistan began on October 7, 2001 and are ongoing. The U.S. has successfully toppled the hostile, terrorist-supporting Taliban government, and efforts to find and defeat the last remaining members of the al Qaeda network continue. Although the precise air strikes in Afghanistan were meant to help sustain international support by demonstrating U.S. concern for minimizing collateral damage, it has proved difficult to project an image of a clean, surgical war. For example, many Pakistani volunteers who were incensed at the perceived brutality of the bombings crossed the border and helped compensate for initial Taliban casualties. Now, more than ever, experts agree that coalition building is of the greatest importance, as it may be difficult to sustain long-term public support for military action.

Youth Involvement

On January 16, 1995, PBS's NewsHour aired a program entitled "The Selling of the Army." In the feature, army officers discussed the difficulties of recruiting the youth of America to enlist with interventions like those in Bosnia on the horizon. "I think the average young kid of today really doesn't see the military as an avenue for the American dream. The Cold War is over, life is good, why do they need to join the military?" said army recruiter Colonel Lisle Brook. Without an archenemy like the Soviet Union to inspire young people to fight in defense of American ideals, the army was left with smaller enlistment numbers.[xxv]

According to a study conducted for the Department of Defense Manpower Center, enlistment among young men decreased after Operation Desert Storm, and in the wake of the disastrous Army Ranger raid of Mogadishu, Somalia in 1993, enthusiasm for enlistment dwindled further.[xxvi]

In an effort to increase youth enlistment, the U.S. military has employed a system of inducements to make service more attractive. Provision of college tuition through the Montgomery GI bill and promises of job training became the primary draw for young people enlisting in the military.[xxvii] Army recruiters have also resorted to more unconventional recruitment tactics. Recruiters have gone into high schools under the guise of substitute teachers and coaches in an effort to more effectively recruit America's youth.[xxviii] The U.S. military has definitely taken an interest in the youth of America–but have young people responded? Even with an advertising budget of $71 million in 1995, Colonel Lisle Brook's greatest hope for rekindling youth involvement in the military was pinned to the success of the intervention in Bosnia.[xxix] An overwhelmingly successful mission, it was thought that Bosnia would trigger a surge of patriotism and increase enthusiasm among youths for enlistment. But it did not prove to be an inspiration for America's youth.

The dramatic effects of the terrorist attack of September 11 seemed to spark youth enthusiasm in a way that recruiters had not seen since the Cold War. A Harris Interactive Survey found that 69% of teenagers supported military intervention in response to the terrorist attack.[xxx] Reports of long lines outside recruitment offices in New York in the weeks after September 11 encouraged military recruiters.[xxxi] It seemed that the enticement to enlist had changed. What used to be primary inducements to service, like college tuition and job training, seemed to have given way to a patriotic spirit and duty. "It's service to country, now," said Army Sgt. 1st Class James Freeman from the Armed Forces Recruiting Center in Times Square.[xxxii]

But despite the apparent surge in support of the military, the overall attitudes of America's youth towards military service changed little. The same Harris Interactive poll that found a substantial amount of support among youth for military intervention found that support decreased significantly when the safety of American military personnel was compromised by intervention.[xxxiii] In another poll entitled Young America: Life After 9/11, only 7% of respondents expressed an increased desire to pursue military service.[xxxiv]

Additionally, there is evidence of a change in attitude of those already in military service in response to September 11. The number of requests for literature about applying for conscientious objector (CO) status fielded by the Central Committee for Conscientious Objectors (CCCO) in Oakland, California increased twelve-fold from August 2001.[xxxv] Conscientious objectors are military personnel who object to engaging in violence of any kind, and the option to claim conscientious objector status is open to all personnel. Often, according to Brian Cross at CCCO, military personnel do not go through with applying for CO status until a conflict like the military action in Afghanistan presents itself.[xxxvi]

While attitudes towards enlistment seem to spark and then quickly die out, anti-war protests tend to rise out of the ashes. Quite aware of the legacy left by alumni, students at University of California at Berkeley formed a peace group in response to the Bush administration's initial intimations at retaliation. Ronald Cruz, a Berkeley student, noted shortly after the attacks:

> We're going to pass flyers out, making a parallel with Vietnam [...]. The U.S. government is making it clear that they're planning a full-scale war. If they're going to do that, we want to make it clear that they're going to get the type of reaction they got in Vietnam. [...] Things are moving very fast [...]. The tragedy really woke up a sector of American society–especially youth and college students.[xxxvii]

Lester Kurtz, a University of Texas at Austin sociology professor, argues, "students have historically been a cornerstone of anti-war movements because they are more available and have a lower risk of getting involved in something that could turn potentially risky."[xxxviii] However, other universities that lacked such a strong anti-war activist past have been unable to make progress as quickly as UC-Berkeley. Youth peace activism, though logical because of the nature of student life, has remained dormant since its heyday during the Vietnam War. U.S. military action in response to September 11 seems to have created an impetus for a resurgence of anti-war activity on college campuses across the country.

However, the results from a Gallup poll taken just months after September 11 might caution against believing that too great a change in attitude or interest in military action, either for or against, has occurred. Though interest of the general population in "military and defense issues" after the terrorist attacks was up to 57% in October 2001 from 26% January 2001, interest had already waned to 42% by January 2002.[xxxix] It would seem that events like United We March on April 20, 2002 in Washington, D.C. must be evidence of increased interest in military activity, but only for a minority of the nation's youth. Despite the expectations for dramatic changes in youth perception and involvement in military interests, it would appear that the pre-September 11 trend of increased indifference continues.

Katharine, age 19
Columbia, SC
Princeton University

How has your view of U.S. military presence/action/intervention in foreign countries changed since September 11?

I don't believe my view of U.S. military intervention has changed significantly. I am certainly more supportive of the action in Afghanistan than of previous actions in Bosnia, Somalia, or even in Iraq during the Gulf War. However, I would ascribe this to the fact that I believe Afghanistan to be a tragically necessary exception to the general rule that U.S. forces should not intervene in a foreign country except pursuant to a declaration of war by the government of that country. I consider what was done in Afghanistan to be an unusual form of self-defense, but self-defense nonetheless.

Where my views on intervention have changed is with respect to my expectation of situations like this one arising. Before September 11, I would have thought it very unlikely that the U.S. could be justified in invading a country whose government had not declared war on us. Now I expect this circumstance to come up again, though I certainly hope it will not. I think the post-September 11 world will be a more confusing one in terms of knowing when one is at war and whom one is actually fighting—whether the terrorist group or the government sponsoring it should be the target, for instance. This, in my opinion, will require even greater vigilance on the part of the U.S. government and military establishment in differentiating between situations in which intervention is necessary and ones in which it is unnecessary and may very well be harmful. So, my view of intervention has not changed, but the reality of global terrorism has forced me to redefine my categories.

How has your view of the U.S. military as an institution changed?

My view of the U.S. military has not changed so much as my suspicions have been confirmed. I have suspected for some time now that the Pentagon does not have the power, vis-à-vis Congress and the White House, that it did some decades ago. I would cite Vietnam as a turning point, but I'm not sure that was the only factor. I saw very clearly in the Afghan action that the White House, specifically Bush's foreign policy advisors and their associates at the State Department, was in charge of what the military did. The administration was extremely careful to keep American casualties to a minimum and to avoid atrocities and tactics that might be construed as human rights violations. This had to do with maintaining domestic support for an undeclared war and with keeping the international coalition together. I got the impression that the action was primarily a political one, with only a few simple-to-understand military components. After all, bin Laden has not yet been captured, and despite the many jokes circulating about his evasion of capture, it has not proved detrimental to the administration's goals. And yet one would think that that would have been the first objective of any military operation. I was thus left after September 11 wondering what the future role of the military establishment would be in military policy-making and strategizing, if any.

Would you be willing to serve in the military? If not, would you consider serving in some sort of non-combatant support role?

I would serve in the military only as a non-combatant. My unwillingness to serve in a combatant role is the consequence of personal convictions and has not changed since September 11. However, I believe I would be more willing to support the military in some capacity now than I would have at this time last year. This is due in some part to an increase in the abstract feeling of national patriotism but is mostly related to my above views on intervention; I feel that U.S. military intervention is more likely to be justifiable now than before, simply because of the kinds of conflicts that will arise. This is not to say that I approve of the expanded "War on Terror" unless another attack is made on American soil or directly targeting American civilians abroad. But I do believe that I would be more willing now to serve in a support role for an action of whose necessity and rectitude I did not necessarily approve. Whether that is the result of the abstract patriot-ism mentioned above or of some conception of a greater need for mili-tary force in the post-September 11 international system, I can't really say.

Do you feel that you have had access to sufficient information about military action and policy post 9/11? Why or why not (is it because the media has not provided enough info, you feel that the government is restricting information because of security concerns, you simply have not followed the issues because you don't have time, etc.)?

I don't doubt that the government is restricting information to some extent, but that doesn't particularly bother me, as it strikes me as a necessary step during a conflict of this sort. While it is important to avoid massacres and other unsavory actions such as those undertaken on occasion without the public's knowledge in Vietnam, I feel that there is less of a need for transparency in a democracy's military policy than in its economic policy, its civilian justice system, and its decision-making mechanisms.

That being said, I think much of the blame for Americans' lack of understanding of the military's role must be put at the feet of the media. The press has focused on the glitzy, jet-setting foreign policy of Powell and Rice, often ignoring the military aspect of the "War on Terrorism." When military matters are addressed, the discussion is often limited to on-the-ground actions in Afghanistan–mostly the very important but not all-eclipsing question of whether U.S. troops have committed human rights violations in Afghan villages. There is very little emphasis, as far as I can tell, on the military plans for expanding the "War on Terrorism," as Bush has called for, on U.S. intervention in the Philippines and military advisors in Georgia, and on the military implications of the threatened unilateralism.

Again, I think it's actually less important that the press cover these sorts of issues than that they give the public a glimpse into the political machinations of the U.S. and its allies—especially given the fact that a good portion of accurate and interesting information about the military's role is classified. When facts are few and far between, the press tends to start filling in the holes with less-than-reliable coverage, and I am glad this is not happening in the coverage of U.S. military involvement as much as it conceivably could happen. Thus, as much as I am irked by the lack of information coming from the media, I realize that the alternative could be far worse.

As a whole are you more or less interested in military policy after 9/11?

I would say that I am more interested.

Tyler, age 22
Albuquerque, NM
United States Military Academy
2nd LT Field Artillery

When should the U.S. intervene militarily? Should they do so only when attacked directly? On behalf of other nations? For humanitarian reasons (prevent genocide, encourage democracy, bring down an authoritarian regime)? Explain.

The politics involved in U.S. military intervention is often deeper than many believe. In the world that we live in today, it is no longer a single massive army that we are worried about having to defend ourselves against like the big Red Army of the past. The enemy today has taken a form that I do not think that we have completely recognized yet. This ominous enemy creates a difficult situation when attempting to pinpoint a good reason to enter a conflict. In the military, we have to be willing and ready to act whenever and wherever the President asks us to enforce U.S. policy. It is not our job to criticize or second guess any decisions, but it is our job to understand the situation that we are sending our soldiers into and the implications of our being there. Subjects like religion, common courtesy, and knowledge of the conflict are all important as we are representing what the United States stands for in a foreign land. This is a very roundabout way of saying that the military is willing and ready whenever the President and the Nation calls on it.

If overt operations cannot be used, should the U.S. employ covert military operations to achieve objectives? What types of covert action would be acceptable? (e.g. Would assassination of dictators be permissible?)

Covert operations are often needed to strike at the enemy's center of gravity (COG). This center of gravity is the center point of their ability to fight. In past times the COG has been the economy of a nation and the army that defends that nation. Now the COG has become stealth and sometimes impossible to pick up. With the decentralized organization of terrorist groups there is often no large force that is identifiable and covert operations become increasingly important. The types of covert operations to be conducted must be left up to those making the big decisions. Again, politics comes into play and there must be deliberation on what lines we are willing to cross in these operations. The United States has an image of democratic ideals that must be upheld to keep its standing in the world. Its leaders are trained to enforce these ideals to the highest of standards. As it stands now the U.S. has a policy not to assassinate leaders of other nations. Until this policy is changed or the opinion of the American people allows for these types of actions to take place, the military must rely on alternative means of power projection to accomplish their goals.

When should the U.S. withdraw from its military actions in other countries?

Again, this is another question that must be decided by the upper echelons of leadership without the questioning of subordinates. The subordinates must be willing and able to uphold the same standard of conduct throughout the entire time that they are deployed to a region. It is important to be able to explain to the soldiers the reasons why they are deployed and the rationale for them to stay for an undetermined amount of time. The underlying principle is that the United States must have the forces that are willing to fulfill their duty to their country to achieve the goals set forth by the administration. However, this military force cannot be at all places at once. We must ensure that our forces are not spread too thin and that we are able to accomplish our missions with the given amounts of soldiers in the different theaters of operations.

What do you think was the U.S.'s most successful military intervention? Least successful? Why?

It is not easy to project a powerful force halfway around the world and win decisive battles. The Gulf War campaign was the major battle of our [generation's] time. The Army showed that it was a powerful force and could overwhelm an enemy quickly and decisively. The fact that we were able to destroy Hussein's fighting force and cripple their will to fight spoke highly of the preparedness of our force. I think this quote from the Wall Street Journal sums it up the best: "Before the Gulf War started, the Iraqi Army was the fourth largest in the world. Now, it's the second largest army in Iraq."[xl] The least successful is difficult to define. Many conflicts have great smaller achievements even when the larger picture has been lost. I do not think that it is my place to put my finger on the map in this matter because I am sure that I do not know the finer points that may make these operations a success in the eyes of administration.

What do you hope the U.S. will achieve through military intervention in Afghanistan? If you oppose military intervention in Afghanistan, what would you propose for U.S. action instead?

The military intervention in Afghanistan is the crux of what I have been talking about in the above questions. The fact that there is not a defined force to fight against, or a center of gravity that we can aim our forces at, means that the difficulty of the operation is greatly increased. The military and political leaders have their hands full as they attempt to find the key to this operation. I think that the forces in Afghanistan have done an amazing job at carrying on with their mission even when the fog of war has covered the mission. The U.S. hopes that this intervention into Afghanistan will help root out the terrorist cells that have used this land to fund and launch their attacks. The ability for the United States to protect the freedoms that their citizens demand is the overarching focus.

Adair, age 21
Columbia, SC
Colorado College

How has your view of U.S. military presence/action/intervention in foreign countries changed since September 11?

It hasn't changed that much. I always knew that we liked to get involved in other countries' affairs whether they had anything to do with our country or not. I don't really know whether or not I think that is the right thing to do or not, but I believe that this time intervention was necessary.

How has your view of the U.S. military as an institution changed?

I still believe that they are an incredibly strong and intelligent military force. All the military personnel and everyone that is involved are very brave and extremely patriotic. I don't know if I could say the same thing for myself, however.

Would you be willing to serve in the military? If not, would you consider serving in some sort of non-combatant support role?

I don't think that I could ever be involved with the military or any type of support role involving the military. I think that the military is a good thing for some people and for our country sometimes. I have very different beliefs and ideals than people involved in the military and I don't think that I would function well in that kind of environment.

Do you feel that you have had access to sufficient information about military action and policy post 9/11? Why or why not (is it because the media has not provided enough info, you feel that the government is restricting information because of security concerns, you simply have not followed the issues because you don't have time, etc)?

I feel that I have been sufficiently informed of what is going on if what the media says is actually true. I'm sure that there is a great deal of information out there that we are not allowed access to, most likely for *good* reasons. But if I actually follow what's going on then I usually feel pretty well informed about the situation.

As a whole are you more or less interested in military policy after 9/11?

I'm still pretty indifferent about the whole military thing. I guess that I'm slightly more interested than before.

David, age 20
San Diego, CA
Boston College
Marine Corps Officer Candidate

When should the U.S. intervene militarily? Should they do so only when attacked directly? On behalf of other nations? For humanitarian reasons (prevent genocide, encourage democracy, bring down an authoritarian regime)? Explain.

The United States should intervene militarily when American interests are threatened (resources, embassies, etc.). It is difficult to say whether the United States should use its military to intervene on the behalf of other nations. I believe that if we are bound by treaty or alliance, then the use of America's armed forces is appropriate. I think it is very difficult to judge whether it is appropriate to use the military to partake in humanitarian missions. On the one hand, all nations must share the planet. This is an inescapable fact. How countries treat each other certainly has repercussions on the future (World War I and Germany, for example). For the limited purpose of preventing genocide, I believe that it is entirely appropriate to deploy armed forces. I do not believe that it is appropriate to deploy armed forces to encourage democracy or to topple authoritarian regimes. The reason is that the definitions for both causes of action change based on national sentiment or the opinions of the nation's leaders at the time. For example, I believe that American military interventions in Central and South America have had disastrous effects on the people of those regions, and all took place in the name of encouraging democracy or overthrowing totalitarian regimes. In reality, this kind of action has proven to be horrifically counterproductive despite the best intentions of our leaders.

If overt operations cannot be used, should the U.S. employ covert military operations to achieve objectives? What types of covert action would be acceptable? (e.g. Would assassination of dictators be permissible?)

If overt operations cannot be used, the U.S. should employ covert operations for the sole purpose of protecting specific and tangible interests (citizens, resources, etc.). Covert operations for the purpose of creating civil disturbance or political instability are not directly related enough to specific interests to justify their use. I am answering this under the assumption that overt operations would not be approved by the global community and that would be why the U.S. would have to use covert tactics.

When should the U.S. withdraw from its military actions in other countries?

The U.S. should withdraw its forces when its specific interests have been sufficiently secured against future possible threats. I do not believe that U.S. troops should be engaged in peacekeeping missions unless they are engaged in an operation that requires their presence to deter genocide (i.e. if there is one particularly powerful faction that actively seeks to eliminate a significantly smaller/weaker faction that does not have means to retaliate).

What do you think was the U.S.'s most successful military intervention? Least successful? Why?

I think that the U.S.'s most successful military intervention was in the Persian Gulf. The U.S. had specific interests that it needed to protect for the security and prosperity of the nation and it successfully defended those interests. The engagement was not prolonged. Soldiers were not placed in a peacekeeping role, which is important because it means they were not placed in harms way for an objective not directly related to the United States' interests. I believe that the U.S.'s least successful military invasion is an ongoing one. U.S. military intervention in Colombia and Central America as part of the "War on Drugs" costs the nation billions of dollars and places servicemen in direct harm for an unachievable objective. This intervention is unsuccessful on a number of levels beyond the physical well-being of special forces. It has failed to produce any noticeable results despite having been carried out for so many years. It has perpetuated war and strife in developing countries, where peace is vital.

What do you hope the U.S. will achieve through military intervention in Afghanistan? If you oppose military intervention in Afghanistan, what would you propose for U.S. action instead?

I hope that the U.S. will achieve its objective of eliminating the al Qaeda terrorist network. I hope that the achievement of this objective will bring peace to a region that has not had a moment to catch its breath in many years. I hope that the long-term effects of U.S. intervention include better relations with the Middle East and the formation of a nation that recognizes the importance of individual rights.

Amy, age 22
Victoria, TX
Longy School of Music

When should the U.S. intervene militarily? Should they do so only when attacked directly? On behalf of other nations? For humanitarian reasons (prevent genocide, encourage democracy, bring down an authoritarian regime)? Explain.

A country as wealthy and powerful as the U.S. has a certain responsibility to the rest of the world to preserve human dignity and equality. It's much like wealthy individuals and corporations within the U.S that are conscience-bound to help those that are less fortunate. We gain nothing by ignoring the problems of other countries, because problems infect other areas of the world; we're not immune to the troubles of other countries, as 9/11 clearly demonstrated. But more importantly, we have a responsibility not to profit from the misfortunes of other countries…I wonder if this is more the source of the problem, that perhaps rather than marching in with guns and threats, we should repair from the inside what is actually causing a lot of outside damage. It seems like the U.S has been very hesitant to take responsibility for their role in perpetuating the animosity of other countries. As individuals, we're kind of microcosms of the world's problems, with our inability to communicate or look within ourselves and solve our own problems. It's sort of like treating the symptom and not the source, and therefore aggravating the problem further, so that any treatment becomes impossible. I feel conflicted about even using the word humanitarian in the same sentence as military.

If overt operations cannot be used, should the U.S. employ covert military operations to achieve objectives? What types of covert action would be acceptable? (e.g. Would assassination of dictators be permissible?)

Well, depending on what day you ask me…I can't really say that I promote violence of any sort, covert or overt. I'm not sure that it does any good for healing and for controlling the real problem. As a temporary solution, though, it might be absolutely necessary at some point and I'd hate not to have the option. I'm so glad that I'm not the one making these decisions…the whole thing makes me want to cry and curl into a fetal position.

When should the U.S. withdraw from its military actions in other countries?

I guess the U.S. should withdraw when it is putting innocent people in death's way, or if the threat of nuclear war is looming. If not defeated, however, it should definitely stay, to help repair that country's wounds.

What do you think was the U.S.'s most successful post-Cold War military intervention? Least successful? Why?

I guess it depends on how you qualify the word successful. The Gulf War was by most accounts "successful," but Hussein is still at large. I don't really have a strong sense of any of them being really successful, other than in a temporary way. The intervention that seems to really help is not militaristic, but humanitarian.

What do you hope the U.S. will achieve through military intervention in Afghanistan? If you oppose military intervention in Afghanistan, what would you propose for U.S. action instead?

I hope, since the U.S. is already there, that mainly they bring aid and relief to the innocent people in Afghanistan, and that these forces are stopped with as little bloodshed as possible. How this could be accomplished, I have no idea.

Chapter 5:

An Emerging Agenda

Since the early 1990's youth awareness of a global community has manifested itself through a demonstrated willingness among young people to work towards securing global human rights: Thousands of students rally in support of universal ratification of the United Nations Declaration of the Rights of a Child; students in American high schools gather weekly to discuss international police brutality; a college sophomore from Wisconsin travels to Nigeria to work for the Peace Corps. Young Americans, driven by an idealistic sense of internationalism, are seeking to effect international change by transcending regular political channels, a trend that markedly differs from youth nationalism during World War II or the hostility, anger, and sense of loss felt towards Vietnam.

But despite youth awareness of international issues, students who seek to affect international change tend to pursue activities that most closely resemble community service rather than embrace engagement in the international political system. Although young people may call on government for immediate solutions to international crises, they fail to engage these problems at a foundational and institutional level, resulting in the continuation of the problems they seek so ardently to address.

Part of the problem is that, while young people seek to combat human rights violations, government policy often contradicts their hopes and ideals. When it comes to donating its vast wealth to developing nations, the United States lags behind much of the developed world. In 2001 it donated 0.1 percent of its GDP ($11 billion) abroad in the form of foreign aid. While President Bush proposed increasing that figure by nearly 50 percent to $16 billion in the year 2006, European

Union member nations have proposed donating 0.39 percent of their own GDPs by that same date.

Moreover, the United States' reluctance to intervene in instances of blatant human rights violations such as the massacres in Rwanda and Sierra Leone during the mid-1990s underscores the point that the difficult realities of U.S. policy-making stand in stark contrast to the idealism of America's youth. While the Clinton administration showed an interest in preventing human suffering in Bosnia, Kosovo, and Somalia, many young activists felt that such interventions were insufficient and, more importantly, too late. UN Secretary General Kofi Annan did not hesitate to address the real cause of the lengthy and disarrayed western response to the Serbian crisis in Srebrenica:

> The failure in Srebrenica is our collective failure. It is a failure of the international community…It wasn't that the international community, the nations of the world, did not have the 34,600 men. But none had the will to make them available for the task we had at hand…We cannot blame those idealistic young men and women, who sign on for peacekeeping operations and are not given the tools to do their work, for our mistakes.

In a September 2000 hearing of the Congressional Subcommittee on International Operation and Human Rights, chairman Representative Christopher H. Smith (R-NJ) highlighted the failures of UN peacekeeping missions in Srebrenica and Rwanda, and the difficulties of maintaining order in East Timor and Sierra Leone. In the first two missions, peacekeeping forces proved especially impotent in the face of fighting and genocide, according to Smith.[xli] Echoing the complaints of the UN's own analysis of its work, Smith pointed to a lack of clear rules of engagement, ill-equipped troops, and technological and logistical deficiencies. Ultimately, he warned against increasing funding for a larger international army that, in his view, has proven ineffective in the past and would pose an increasing threat to national sovereignty.[xlii]

On the other hand, UN peacekeeping forces have the potential to play a crucial role in the process of nation-building, an issue that has taken on an increasing urgency after the war in Afghanistan. While the traditional roles of peacekeeping forces are preventing violence and monitoring cease-fires, these personnel are increasingly performing the functions of "peace-builders," "from protecting and delivering humanitarian assistance, to helping former opponents carry out complicated peace agreements; from assisting with the demobilization of former fighters and their return to normal life, to supervising and conducting elections; from training civilian police, to monitoring respect for human rights and investigating alleged violations."[xliii] The United Nations has especially seized on the ability of peace-keeping missions to fulfill nation-building duties because of the wariness of skeptics like Smith. Where the phrase "nation-building" is politically-loaded, "peace-building" seems to describe a more innocuous method of dealing with failed states.

Nonetheless, critics of UN intervention seem to have won the day, at least with U.S. foreign-policymakers. In many respects, Smith's criticisms highlight the U.S. government's essentially realist approach to foreign policy, which was dominant throughout the 1990s, even despite the Clinton administration's rhetorical appeal to humanitarian intervention. The Somalia crisis exemplifies the disconnect this approach has created between young people and the decisions of their political leaders. In 1990, the United States provided Somalia with $579 million of arms in exchange for American bases in Somalia, which was a key strategic asset because of its location next to the Suez Canal, a major shipping lane with ready access to oil-rich Saudi Arabia and the Persian Gulf. Without those arms, it is debatable whether the Somali civil war would even have erupted. That U.S. food aid was withheld for two months prior to U.S. troops landing to rescue Somalia from starvation also renders the solely compassionate message hard to believe. Today, seven years after United Nations withdrawal and eight years after American troops left the country, the civil war between rival warlords, while smaller in scale, continues to plague the peace in Mogadishu, confirming young people's suspicions of government's inability to effectively implement systemic reform.

What do we owe the rest of the world in an era of globalization, disintegrating borders, and cultural homogenization? To what extent do we see our neighbors both near and far as partners or competitors for the present and future? The limited record of young people who have begun to think about issues such as these is in fact quite encouraging. In response to the growing crisis in Africa surrounding the proliferation of AIDS, a group of students concerned about the issue formed in 2001 to do what it could to change U.S. policy. The Student Global Aids Campaign (SGAC) represents the largest network of high school and college students devoted to the worldwide fight against AIDS. Its mission is to increase U.S. AIDS-related foreign aid to $2.5 billion through various forms of political activism including lobbying the federal government, forming student protests, increasing student awareness, and promoting media coverage of the issue. This kind of organization represents the very best of what American youth can offer both the country and the world. In fact, due to the efforts of AIDS activists like the SGAC–and the direct intervention of the rock-star Bono of U2–Senator Jesse Helms of North Carolina, the former chair of the Senate Foreign Relations Committee, has proposed legislation to increase foreign aid for AIDS-related issues by $500 million.

This example represents the potential for America's current generation of youth to make a significant impact on the world around them. This will require both an awareness of the issues and an understanding that political action can and does achieve results. Certainly, the SGAC cannot claim responsibility for a victory in the fight against AIDS, but its mere effort represents a critical shift in the right direction for this generation, both in terms of mindset and attitude. Not only are these students deeply aware of issues of international concern, they understand that the United States has significant responsibilities to the rest of the world. This shift in awareness from local and national issues to those of the entire world is crucial for our generation. Only by coming to understand how our interests are inextricably linked to those of our neighbors can we come to form an effective foreign policy in the best interest of our country and the rest of the world.

An increase in awareness of international issues must start with small groups of highly motivated and informed young people and build into larger movements. The formation of grassroots student groups such as SGAC is the very mechanism to create such an effect. Our generation cannot depend on a heightened awareness from the evening news; rather, we must learn from our peers and engage these issues within larger groups. While grassroots movements do not always translate into real-world change, such movements always irrevocably transform the mindsets of its members, creating the proper attitude and awareness necessary for our generation to successfully lead the country towards more effective international relationships.

Conclusion

While September 11 initiated a noticeable spike in levels of civic awareness among high-school and college-aged Americans, it seems disturbingly clear that this interest is fading more rapidly with every passing day. Fear and grief inspired young Americans to join their fellow citizens in a surge of patriotism and pride, and simultaneously created a desire to stay informed about world events. But as the intensity of these emotions recedes, America is losing its grip on the one positive impact September 11 might have had on the future of our nation, that very change among youth attitudes towards politics. Young people have fallen back into an abyss of disinterest and are returning to their previous *modus operandi*: community service and direct volunteerism. A year and a half after September 11, larger systemic problems have not been addressed: corporate malfeasance runs amok, single-issue news coverage dominates the airwaves, money continues to determine political decisions, and a choking centrism guised as bipartisanship locks American politics more securely at ground zero than ever before. Young voters, tired of being treated as consumers rather than citizens, turned out to the 2002 midterm elections in predictably disappointing numbers. This seems hardly surprising given the dishonorable fashion in which candidates conducted their campaigns, which were noteworthy primarily for their vitriolic attacks on other candidates' patriotism.

As this political culture slowly returns to dominate our conception of politics and government, our belief in government as a powerful force for meaningful change vanishes. September 11 was not the defining moment for our generation. We suffered with our country emotionally, but did not participate actively. There was no draft. There were no Liberty Bonds. There was no social mobilization. Unlike the Greatest Generation, we neither fought abroad nor contributed at home. Unlike the Baby Boomers, we neither protested nor sacrificed. "Generation 9/11" neither contributed on the battlefield nor on the home front. September 11 was not Pearl Harbor; it was not World War II; it was not Vietnam.

September 11 sparked a period of unprecedented awareness of domestic and international affairs whose influence still lingers. But political leaders are failing to channel this urgency into meaningful modes of political activity. During World War II and Vietnam, leaders like Franklin Roosevelt and John F. Kennedy inspired young Americans to embrace the possibilities of civic participation and to accept their responsibilities to themselves and their fellow citizens. We, on the other hand, were told to return to our normal lives, to continue shopping, to take a trip to Disney World. We were not asked to help our country, and we were not compelled to believe that our participation in governmental service might contribute to our society or our security.

But while the immediate months after September 11 may have provided the best opportunity for instilling a civic culture into America's youth, all hope is not yet lost. Young people are still interested in channeling their energies to make tangible differences; indeed, 86% believe they have the qualities and character to lead America in the future. But for our generation to become engaged in government, barriers to entry must be demolished and the culture of politics must be changed. Though proposing and implementing tangible reforms will meet institutional and political resistance, there *are* clear ways to spark the engagement of our generation:

Loan forgiveness. Federal and state governments should offer loan forgiveness or signing bonuses to qualified students who commit to government work for three to five years after college. Fully 93% of college students believe that such a program would be effective in getting them more interested in politics and public service.

<u>Salary Levels</u>. The low level of government salaries actively deters young people from careers in public service. Americans were shocked to find that the heroes of September 11, firefighters and policemen, were paid dismal salaries; yet across the board, all government employees are paid poorly for the services they provide to our society and country. 91% of students feel that if salaries and benefits afforded to government employees were comparable to those in the private sector, they would be more involved in politics and government.

<u>Military Opportunities</u>. Students want to serve their country, but many do not wish to participate in combat directly. The U.S. Military should offer an opportunity for young people to enlist for 2 to 5 years in non-combat areas like policy and communications; 79% of young people believe this would be an effective way to draw them into political service.

<u>Contact</u>. Young people need more direct contact with elected officials, candidates, and political institutions. 62% of people under 30 say they were never asked to consider working in government while in high school or college. If asked, nearly one-quarter of students would participate in political campaigns—a significant figure given that only 9% were actually involved in 2002. 92% of students believe this would be an effective measure to combat their noninvolvement. Leaders should therefore speak more often with schools, colleges, and community groups where they can listen to and address young people's concerns, while informing them of the opportunities that government service provides.

<u>Curriculum</u>. Our education system does not place enough focus on civic responsibility. In addition to teaching a general civics curriculum, public schools must teach the basics on how students can get involved

in politics and political activism. Without a sound education in American political institutions and processes, young people cannot become more active. Additionally, colleges and universities should promote political engagement by partnering with local and state governments and offering academic credit to students who participate in politics. 94% of young people believe this would encourage political activism.

Of course, these specific policy proposals are not enough in and of themselves to eradicate the kind of civic malaise that adults identify with our generation. Without broader and more substantial reforms in American political culture, it is unlikely that young people will transform themselves into a body of responsible, informed, and compassionate citizens and leaders. A decisive shift must be made away from a political structure that attempts to influence and persuade from the top down and that is concerned above all with marketing itself in order to ensure its self-perpetuation. Young people spend their lives inundated in a culture of advertising, which has extended itself into the political realm. Choosing between commercial pop CDs and between political candidates has taken on a dangerously similar flavor, and this is a connection young people are quick to perceive. But politics is not a sport or a passing form of entertainment. Our generation cares too much about real people and the issues that affect them to waste their time on what they see as an endless batch of would-be leaders who are too busy responding to polling data to actually lead. This perception is born less out of apathy and more out of disgust. A lack of courage has inspired a lack of engagement. And it has led to what may be the truly greatest tragedy of the 21st century, our generation's disavowal of the political realm.

The Institute of Politics Survey of Student Attitudes

A NATIONAL SURVEY OF COLLEGE UNDERGRADUATES

Conducted October 18-27, 2002

A study by
The Institute of Politics
John F. Kennedy School of Government
Harvard University

The Institute of Politics
Harvard University
79 JFK Street
Cambridge, MA 02138
(617) 495-1360

Key Findings

Students are engaged in their community but are not involved in political activities.

- Nearly two-thirds of college students say they have recently volunteered in community service; 89% of this group volunteered in high school. Fewer than ten percent of undergraduates nationwide have volunteered on a political campaign.
- Students believe volunteerism is an effective form of public service to solve problems on both the local and national level.
- Community service is familiar territory for college students. Eighty percent of undergraduates performed direct service in high school.

While unlikely to be involved in politics, students are following politics and consider it to be important.

- Thirty-two percent of students were registered to vote and definitely planned to do so in the 2002 midterm elections. This figure is double the midterm turnout rate of their age group.
- Forty-two percent read the newspaper or watch the news on a daily basis and seventy-one percent do so more than once a week. Sixty-eight percent of students report discussing politics and current events with friends and family at least once weekly.
- Two-thirds of respondents consider politics relevant to their lives.
- Students overwhelmingly consider political engagement an effective way of solving important issues both around the country (87%) and in their communities (84%). A majority (56%) disagreed with the claim that political involvement rarely has tangible results.

Students feel highly patriotic and most conditionally support action against Iraq yet are reluctant about the prospect of military service.

- Patriotic sentiment is nearly universal with 90% considering them-selves very or somewhat patriotic. It is one of few figures that remains steady since September 11 although the intensity has dipped.

- A strong majority of students favor US military action against Iraq if UN inspections fail. However, support drops to 18% if the US has to act alone. Twenty-eight percent unconditionally oppose mil-itary action.

- Two-thirds of respondents oppose the idea of reinstating a military draft. If the draft were reinstated, 44% indicated that, if selected, they would seek an alternative to service. Only one-quarter would eagerly serve and 28% would serve with reservation.

After a spike in the aftermath of September 11th, indicators of politi-cal engagement and trust in government are receding toward their 2000 levels.

- Trust in various government institutions is uniformly lower than figures from last year. Trust in Congress, the federal government, the President, and the military have all declined 5 to 11 percent.

- The military remains the most trusted public institution (70% trust to do the right thing all or most of the time), and the President is a distant second with 58%.

- The federal government has held onto a gain in confidence com-pared to two years ago; while down 9% from last year's figure, the trust in federal government remains 15% higher than 2000 levels.

- Involvement in both political campaigns and government/issues-based organizations, after nearly doubling between 2000 and 2001, has returned to their 2000 levels.

Traditional student issues are taking a back seat to concerns about foreign policy and terrorism.

- The issues mentioned as the greatest concern to undergraduates are terrorism (33%) and the conflict in Iraq (25%). Domestic issues, such as education and the economy, have lost their traditional prominence among students.
- More than two-thirds of those surveyed are greatly or somewhat concerned about an upcoming terrorist attack in the United States. Eight-two percent report being greatly or somewhat affected in their thinking about national issues following September 11.

Introduction

The students populating college campuses across America are widely seen as a disengaged, dot-com youth, plugged into virtual communities and relatively "unplugged" from the realities of civic life. A perceived lack of enthusiasm for politics among this population of eighteen to twenty-four year olds has caused many to regard the average college student as unwilling to get involved in public service. The intent of The Institute of Politics National Survey of Undergraduates is to assess the fact or fiction of these public perceptions. Our 2002 findings reveal that students are in fact active as volunteers providing service within their communities, yet they remain relatively inactive when it comes to political campaigns and organizations. For today's students there appears to be a distinction between public service and political participation.

Overall, college students are neither apathetic nor uninformed about public issues. Students follow current events, and their public spirit is taking the form of volunteerism. Most are volunteering in their community, and most believe volunteerism is an effective means for addressing problems in their home communities and around the nation. And while the long-term impact of the September 11th attacks on our generation's public attitudes remains a topic of speculation for sociologists and political scientists, our data reveal that 9/11 did not introduce this spirit of community engagement on college campuses, but rather temporarily reinforced a commitment that was already present. In 2001 students responded to the fallout of September with increased levels of volunteerism and heightened trust in the institutions of government and public service. Our 2002 data suggests that although these levels of service and trust have subsided to near their pre-2001 measures, students continue to regard terrorism as the most important issue facing our country. The hoped-for silver lining of 9/11 may not come for students in the form of increased involvement in public service, because many students were already hard at work in their communities well before last September.

Interest and activism, however, do not promise political involvement. With fewer than one tenth of college students participating in campaigns, and only a slightly higher percentage engaged in political organizations or activities, it is clear that students are not seeking to make their mark on the political arena. But according to the survey data, the sparseness of students on the campaign trail is not simply the result of a disinterest or distaste for politics in general. Most college students believe that politics is an effective means for addressing issues facing their community and their nation, and just as many say that they believe political action can have tangible results. Nor are they altogether estranged from the political culture—nearly half of all students believe that they are more or less the same as their peers who are participating in politics.

Overall, the data collected from this 2002 survey suggest that college students have fashioned a political culture in which involvement is not a function of awareness, and civic engagement is not exhibited by marching for a campaign or movement, but is instead service to the underprivileged through an after school session, weekend outing, or spring break mission. For a majority of students, hammering for Habitat for Humanity, donating time to a local soup kitchen, or any other form of volunteerism has become a significant part of the college experience. The gap between high levels of community service and low levels of political engagement among students is a cause for concern, and a call for solutions. Our findings suggest that the remedy to this problem may not come in the form of slick packaging or marketing efforts to make students politically aware—they already are. Students have indicated that they are attuned to the debate and discussion of issues facing their nation and home communities. Instead, students are calling for increased access to current leaders and new opportunities to get acquainted with the practical side of the political system at an early age. Young people are, in our own way, paying attention to political matters, and now we are waiting to see if politics is prepared to pay attention to us.

Mood of American Students

- **Students are nearly split on the direction of the country (45% right direction vs. 44% wrong track).** African American students, however, are more skeptical about the direction of our country.

- Iraq and terrorism weigh heavily on the minds of students. **When asked what issue most concerns them, 33% mentioned a terrorism-related issue and 25% mentioned the crisis in Iraq. Traditional student issues, such as education (7%), jobs/economy (7%) and the environment (1%) were rarely mentioned as the most pressing concern.**

- Patriotism remains high, but less intensely felt than one year ago. **While 90% of students describe themselves as very or somewhat patriotic, the intensity of patriotism has waned, with those feeling "very patriotic" down to 33% from 48% a year ago.**

- More than two-thirds of students (69%) believe that the U.S. should act with the support of allies against Iraq if UN inspections fail. Less than one-third of those surveyed believe that the U.S. should take no military action.

- **When asked about a potential draft, 67% of those surveyed oppose the reinstatement of the draft, including 39% who strongly oppose the draft. If the draft were reinstated and the respondent was drafted, 44% would seek an alternative to service.**

- Overall, trust in government institutions is high, although not as high as this time last year. **The military remains the most trusted government institution with 70% trusting it to do the right thing** all or most of the time, followed by the President at 58%. Students are least trustful of large corporations and the media.

- Similarly, participation in political campaigns and government, political or issues-related organizations has fallen after a temporary rise in October 2001.

- Thirty-two percent of undergraduates say they are registered and will definitely vote this November. If turnout reflects this figure, college students will vote at twice the rate of their age group (16.6% turnout for 18 to 24 year olds[1]). **Black students are more likely to be registered and to vote in the upcoming election and they are more likely than other ethnic groups to attend political rallies or demonstrations.**

---

[1] US Census Bureau, Table 1: Reported Voting & Registration, 11/98 Internet Release Date July 19, 2000

Characteristics of the Next Generation of Leaders

- **College students have spare time and are generous in sharing it.** Sixty-seven percent of college students say they have time to be involved in activities outside of school and work, and 61% of college students indicate they have volunteered for community service in the last 12 months. The single greatest predictor of volunteerism in community service is whether the student volunteered in high school (89% of students who participated in community service in the last twelve months had volunteered in high school).

- **Students believe that volunteerism is an effective way of solving important issues facing the country and their community.** Ninety-three percent believe volunteerism is an effective way of solving important issues facing their community; 84% believe community volunteerism is an effective way of solving important issues facing the country as a whole.

- **Similarly, careers in non-profit or community-based organizations are strong contenders for future employment while interest in running for public office is very low.** Sixty-eight percent say they would very or somewhat seriously consider working for a non-profit or community-based organization for some part of their future employment. Fifty-six percent say they would consider working for the government (excluding military) but only 16% of respondents say they would consider running for public office.

- **College students believe politics is relevant, but remain uninvolved in political organizations, demonstrations, or campaigns.** Almost two-thirds of those surveyed (63%) think that politics is relevant to their lives and just over half (56%) believe that politics has tangible results. Most students (87%) believe that political engagement is an effective way of solving important issues facing the country. Eighty-four percent say the same for issues facing the community.

- **Undergraduates are not engaging in the political system.** Only 9% say they have participated in a political campaign in the last 12 months and only 14% say they have participated in a government, political, or issues-related organization in the last 12 months. Eighty percent of students say they have not participated in a political rally or demonstration in the same time period. Factors that influence whether a student engages in political activities include: whether somebody asked them to participate, direct contact with a government official or candidate, and regular discussions about politics and current events with family members while growing up.

- **College students are watching and talking about current events but distrust the media.** Seventy-one percent of college students indicate they read a newspaper or watch the news more than once per week. More than two-thirds of all college students (68%) say they discuss political issues with family and friends more than once per week. Trust in the media to do the right thing all or most of the time, however, is only 12%—the lowest rating of the institutions tested in the survey.

- **On a scale of 0-10, 26% of students feel that the American political system is very sound (8-10) while only 3% of students feel the system is very flawed (0-2).** African American students, however, are less likely than other ethnic groups to rate our political system as very sound.

Please rate our political system on a scale of 0-10	Total	Caucasian	Asian	Hispanic	African-American
Flawed (0-2)	3%	3%	6%	0	8%
Very Sound (8-10)	26%	28%	18%	35%	17%

- **African Americans students are more politically active and more skeptical of the system.** While African American students are much less likely to expect tangible results from political involvement than their white colleagues (46% and 60% respectively), they are the most likely ethnic group to vote and are more likely to be involved in political organizations (28%) than the general student population (20%). African American skepticism towards institutions seems to be reserved for the civilian government: they are less likely than students in general to trust the federal government (38% to 51%) and Congress (42% to 52%), while trusting the ethics of the military, large corporations, and the media to the same extent as other ethnic groups.

Motivating Students into Public Service

- **Barriers to engagement need to be lowered.** Eighty-six percent of college students indicate they need more practical information about politics before getting involved. Almost nine in ten students (89%) say volunteering in the community is easier than volunteering in politics.

- **High schools need to foster and emphasize political activity to build a foundation for political engagement similar to the promotion of community service.** Eighty percent of undergraduates volunteered for community service while in high school and eighty-nine percent of those who are currently volunteering had done so in high school. In general, 64% of all students have volunteered for community service in the last twelve months.

- **Bring a friend! Students need to ask friends to vote and become politically active.** On a scale of 0 to 10 (0=definitely not attend; 10=definitely attend), more than one-third of respondents are very likely (8-10) to attend a political rally or demonstration on an issue they support if a friend asked them. Furthermore, 24% of students would very likely volunteer on a political campaign if asked by a friend. One-quarter of the undergraduate population translates to almost three million young voters who could be mobilized by appeals from their peers.

- **Elected officials need to connect with young people and government agencies should actively recruit on college campuses.** Ninety-two percent of college students say more direct contact with elected officials, political candidates, and others in government would be a very or somewhat effective way of getting students involved in politics. Likewise, 90% say campus recruitment by government agencies would be an effective method of motivating students into public service.

Trust in large corporations to do the right thing all or most of the time is extremely low compared to the federal government (19% corporations vs. 51% federal government). Paradoxically, seventy percent of respondents (31% very+39% somewhat seriously) say they would consider working for a large corporation after graduation while 56% (18% very+38% somewhat) say they would consider working for the government.

- **Athletes, actors, and entertainers can influence young people to become involved in politics and public service, particularly minority students.** Seventy-one percent of respondents believe the involvement of respected celebrities and sports figures would be effective in boosting political engagement. Among African-American and Hispanic students, involvement of role models is seen as particularly effective (80% and 81% respectively).

- **Politically oriented students are not alienated from other students.** Although only one-fifth of students have recently engaged in politics or a political organization, almost half of the respondents (47%) believe that young people involved in politics are essentially the same as themselves. In community service, on the other hand, the number of students who felt that participants were the same as themselves was roughly equivalent to the number already involved (68% and 61%, respectively). This discrepancy may represent an opportunity for growth in student political involvement that is not reflected when it comes to community service.

Methodology

This survey is the third in an annual project at Harvard University's Institute of Politics ("IOP"). The first survey was conducted in April 2000, the second in October 2001, and the third in October 2002. For tracking purposes, a number of questions remain the same throughout the surveys, while the majority of questions change from year to year. All three surveys were designed by a team of Harvard undergraduates working with the staff and Fellows of Harvard's Institute of Politics and with John DellaVolpe of Schneiders/Della Volpe/Schulman ("S/D/S"), a national opinion research firm.

S/D/S executed the survey through telephone interviews with a random sample of undergraduate students at four-year colleges and universities in the United States. A total of 1,200 interviews lasting 19 minutes each were conducted between October 18 and October 26, 2002. The margin of error is+/-2.8% at a 95% confidence level. For smaller subgroups, the margin of error is larger.

WORKING GROUP

DAN GLICKMAN, IOP DIRECTOR	GORDON LI, DIRECTOR OF OUTREACH
Cathy McLaughlin, Executive Director	John DellaVolpe, S/D/S

Peter Buttigieg '04, Project Co-Chair	Daniel Margolskee '05
Ryan Rippel '04, Project Co-Chair	Venu Nadella '04
Rahul Rohatgi '03, Project Co-Chair	James Paquette '06
Jonathan Chavez '05	Peter Schwartzstein '04
Guillermo Coronado '05	Genevieve Sheehan '05
Edward Couch '05	Ganesh Sitaraman '04
Andy Frank '05	Elise Stefanik '06
Joey Hanzich '06	Rob Varady '06
Nicholas Ma '05	Lixin Xu '06

The Institute of Politics

The Institute of Politics began operation in 1966 with an endowment from the Kennedy Library Corporation. A living memorial to President John F. Kennedy, the Institute seeks to unite students, particularly undergraduates, with academicians, politicians, activists, and policymakers on a non-partisan basis and to stimulate and nurture their interest in public service and leadership. For more information, please visit www.iop.harvard.edu.

Washington, DC • Boston
www.sdsprime.com

Harvard University–Institute of Politics
OCTOBER 18–OCTOBER 27, 2002

n=1,200 College Undergraduates

MARGIN OF ERROR=+/-2.8% AT THE 95% CONFIDENCE LEVEL

• •

NOTE: PERCENTAGES MAY NOT ADD UP TO 100% DUE TO ROUNDING.*INDICATES PERCENTAGES OF LESS THAN 0.5%

Introduction:

Hello, my name is (INTERVIEWER) from Schneiders/Della Volpe/Schulman, a national opinion research company. Today we are conducting a very important survey of college students, and would like very much to include your opinions. I think you will find it interesting. I assure you that your answers will be kept completely confidential and this is not a sales call–we are only interested in your opinions. Before I begin, I just need to ask you a few questions to make sure that you qualify...

1. Are you currently attending an undergraduate student at a four-year college or university?

	2002	2001	2000
Yes	100%	100%	100%

2. Are you a United States citizen?

	2002	2001	2000
Yes	100%	100%	100%

3. Could you please tell me your age? [2]

	2002	2001	2000
Under 18	4%	3%	2%
18-20	60%	65%	58%
21-24	36%	32%	40%

4. Are you registered to vote? [Sample=voting age]

	2002	2001 (n=1187)	2000 (n=781)
Yes	70%	75%	73%
No	29%	24%	27%
DK/Refused	1%	1%	1%

5. [IF "NO" IN Q-4] Are you planning on registering to vote before the election in November?

	2002
Yes	45%
No	45%
DK/Refused	10%

---

[2] Differences in response to the age question is due to the fact that the 2000 survey was conducted in April 2001—at the end of the academic year, and the 2001 and 2002 surveys were conducted in October, closer to the beginning.

6. When it comes to voting, do you consider yourself to be affiliated with the Democratic Party, the Republican Party, or are you Independent or Unaffiliated with a major party?

	2002 (n=1200)	2001 (n=982)	2000 (n=567)
Democrat	29%	29%	34%
Republican	26%	31%	28%
Independent/Unaffiliated	40%	39%	33%
Other	1%	-	1%
DK/Refused	4%	1%	5%

7. How likely is it that you will vote in the upcoming election in November? Will you definitely be voting, will you probably be voting, are you 50-50, or do you think you probably won't be voting in the November election?

	2002
Definitely be voting	36%
Probably be voting	24%
50-50	17%
Probably won't vote	21%
DK/Refused	2%

8. **[IF DEFINITELY/PROBABLY VOTING ASK]:** Why are you voting this year? [RECORD VERBATIM]

9. **[IF DEFINITELY/PROBABLY VOTING ASK]:** Why are you probably not voting this year? [RECORD VERBATIM]

10. **[IF 18 or older]** Have you ever voted in an election before?

	2002
Yes	47%
No–But Eligible	30%
No–Not Eligible	23%

We are interested in learning more about some of the activities that students partici-pate in when they are not in school or work.

11. Generally, do you feel like you have enough time to be involved in activities other than schoolwork or a job, or not?

	2002	2001	2000
Have enough time	67%	67%	60%
Do not have enough time	33%	32%	39%
DK/Refused	1%	*	1%

Some students have more time than others to get involved in non-scholastic activities. For each of the following please tell me if you happen to have participated in that activity in the last 12 months–and then if you have, please tell me how often in the last year you have participated in that activity—weekly, a few times a month, about once a month or less than once a month .

Here is the first one:_____ Have you _____ in the last 12 months? [IF YES] Did you participate in this activity weekly, a few times a month, about once a month or less than once a month?

	A SERIES		_B SERIES_			
	HAVE PARTICI-PATED	HAVE NOT PARTICI-PATED	WEEKLY	A FEW TIMES A MONTH	ABOUT ONCE A MONTH	LESS THAN ONCE A MONTH
12. Volunteered for community service.	'02 – 61% '01 – 70% '00 - 60%	'02 - 39% '01 – 30% '00 - 41%	'02 - 24% '01 - 11%	'02 - 19% '01 – 10%	'02 - 30% '01 – 27%	'02 - 26% '01 – 21%
13. A government, political or issues-related organization.	'02 – 14% '01 - 28% '00 - 16%	'02 - 86% '01 – 72% '00 - 84%	'02 - 30% '01 - 7%	'02 - 22% '01 – 3%	'02 - 22% '01 – 7%	'02 - 26% '01 – 10%
14. Organized sports or another organization that does not deal with politics or issues.	'02 – 60%	'02 - 40%	'02 - 67%	'02 - 18%	'02 - 11%	'02 - 4%

15. Have you <u>ever</u>   '02 - 9%   '02 - 91%
    volunteered on a
    political campaign?   '01 - 13%   '01 - 87%

                           '00 - 7%   '00 - 94%

16. Have you ever
    attended a political   '02 - 20%   '02 - 80%
    rally or
    demonstration?

17. Imagine that a friend or peer suggests attending a political rally or demonstra-
    tion. Assuming you have some free time and you agree with the issue—how
    likely would you be to agree to attend, using a scale of zero to ten where zero
    means you definitely would NOT attend and ten means you definitely would
    attend.

	2002
Net: Not Attend (0-2)	11%
Definitely Would Not Attend(0)	6%
(1)	2%
(2)	3%
Net: (3-7)	52%
(3)	5%
(4)	4%
(5)	16%
(6)	8%
(7)	19%
Net: Attend (8-10)	37%
(8)	22%
(9)	7%
Definitely Would Attend (10)	8%
Don't Know	*%
Mean	6.18

18. Imagine that a friend or peer suggests volunteering on a political campaign .
    Again, assuming you support the campaign's platform and issues, how likely
    would you be to agree to volunteer, using a scale of zero to ten where zero means

you definitely would NOT volunteer and ten means you definitely would volunteer.

	2002
Net: Not Attend (0-2)	16%
Definitely Would Not Attend(0)	9%
(1)	3%
(2)	5%
Net: (3-7)	59%
(3)	7%
(4)	8%
(5)	18%
(6)	11%
(7)	15%
Net: Attend (8-10)	24%
(8)	13%
(9)	5%
Definitely Would Attend (10)	6%
Don't Know	*%
Mean	5.33

19. Now, imagine that a friend or peer suggests volunteering for community service . How likely would you be to agree to volunteer for community service, using a scale of zero to ten where zero means you definitely would NOT volunteer and ten means you definitely would volunteer.

	2002
Net: Not Attend (0-2)	4%
Definitely Would Not Attend(0)	2%
(1)	*%
(2)	1%
Net: (3-7)	33%
(3)	2%
(4)	2%
(5)	9%
(6)	6%

(7)	13%
Net: Attend (8-10)	64%
(8)	23%
(9)	18%
Definitely Would Attend (10)	22%
Don't Know..	*
Mean	7.65

[ROTATE NEXT 2]

20. Thinking for a moment about people around your age who are involved in community service–would you say they are more or less the same as you, or are they different in some way?

	2002
Same..	68%
Different...	29%
DK/Refused	3%

21. Thinking for a moment about people around your age who are involved in politics–would you say they are more or less the same as you, or are they different in some way?

	2002
Same..	47%
Different...	49%
DK/Refused	5%

Now I am going to read several career or employment choices that people make. After I read each one, please tell me how seriously you have considered–or will consider— each choice for some part of your future employment–very seriously, somewhat seriously, not very seriously or not at all seriously.

[ROTATE QUESTIONS]	VERY SERIOU S-LY	SOME-WHAT SERIOU S-LY	NET: SERIOU S-LY	NOT VERY SERIOU S-LY	NOT AT ALL SERIOU S-LY	NET: NOT SERIOU S-LY	DK/ REFUSED
22. Work for a non-profit orcommunity-based organization	'02 – 18% '01 - 13%	'02 – 50% '01 - 38%	'02 – 68% '01 - 51%	'02 – 21% '01 - 34%	'02 – 11% '01 - 14%	'02 – 31% '01 - 48%	'02 – 1% '01 - *
23. Work for the government – not including military service.	'02 – 18% '01 - 19%	'02 – 38% '01 - 33%	'02 – 56% '01 - 52%	'02 – 21% '01 - 24%	'02 – 22% '01 - 23%	'02 – 44% '01 - 47%	'02 - *% '01 - *
24. Join the military.	'02 – 6% '01 - 3%	'02 – 12% '01 - 14%	'02 – 18% '01 - 17%	'02 – 21% '01 - 19%	'02 – 60% '01 - 64%	'02 – 81% '01 - 83%	'02 - 2% '01 - *
25. Work for a large corporation.	'02 – 31%	'02 – 39%	'02 – 70%	'02 – 16%	'02 – 14%	'02 – 30%	'02 – 1%
26. Work in a short-term national service program such as the Peace Corps, AmeriCorps or Teach for America.	'02 – 12% '01 - 10%	'02 – 31% '01 - 30%	'02 – 42% '01 - 40%	'02 – 27% '01 - 27%	'02 – 29% '01 - 33%	'02 – 57% '01 - 60%	'02 – 1% '01 - *
27. Run for elected office.	'02 – 5% '01 - 6%	'02 – 11% '01 - 18%	'02 – 16% '01 - 24%	'02 – 26% '01 - 23%	'02 – 58% '01 - 53%	'02 – 83% '01 - 76%	'02 - * '01 - *

Which of the following office would you consider running for: [Sample=Seriously Considering run for office]

28. A local office?

	2002	2001
Yes	76%	77%
No	20%	21%
Don't know	3%	2%

29. A state office?

	2002	2001
Yes	71%	58%
No	26%	38%
Don't know	3%	4%

30. A federal office?

	2002	2001
Yes	54%	51%
No	45%	45%
Don't know	1%	3%

Moving on now, I am going to ask you a few questions about political engagement and community volunteerism.

	VERY EFFECT-IVE	S'WHAT EFFECT-IVE	NET: EFFECT-IVE	NOT VERY EFFECT-IVE	NOT AT ALL EFFECT-IVE	NET: NOT EFFECT-IVE	DON'T KNOW
[ROTATE NEXT 2 QUESTIONS]							
31. How effective do you think political engagement is as a way of solving important issues facing the country? Would you say it is very effective, somewhat effective, not very effective or not at all effective?	'02 - 28% '01 - 30%	'02 - 59% '01 - 62%	'02 - 87% '01 - 92%	'02 - 9% '01 - 6%	'02 - 2% '01 - 2%	'02 - 11% '01 - 8%	'02 - 1% '01 - 1%
32. How effective do you think political engagement is as a way of solving important issues facing the community?	'02 - 26% '01 - 20%	'02 - 59% '01 - 56%	'02 - 84% '01 - 76%	'02 - 10% '01 - 21%	'02 - 3% '01 - 2%	'02 - 14% '01 - 23%	'02 - 3% '01 - 1%
[ROTATE NEXT 2 QUESTIONS]	'02 - 38% '01 - 36%	'02 - 46% '01 - 48%	'02 - 84% '01 - 84%	'02 - 12% '01 - 13%	'02 - 2% '01 - 2%	'02 - 14% '01 - 15%	'02 - 1% '01 - 1%
33. How effective do you think community volunteerism is as a way of solving important issues facing the country?							
34. How effective do you think community volunteerism is as a way of solving important issues facing the community?	'02 - 55% '01 - 69%	'02 - 38% '01 - 27%	'02 - 93% '01 - 86%	'02 - 5% '01 - 3%	'02 - 1% '01 - *	'02 - 6% '01 - 3%	'02 - 1% '01 - *

Switching gears, I am going to read you a short list of individuals and institutions, and after I read each one I am going to ask you how much you trust them. Please tell me whether you trust them to do the right thing all of the time, most of the time, some of the time, or never. Here's the first one:

[ROTATE QUESTIONS]	ALL OF THE TIME	MOST OF THE TIME	SOME OF THE TIME	NEVER	DK/ REFUSED
35. The President.	'02 – 15%	'02 – 43%	'02 – 34%	'02 – 8%	'02 – *
	'01 - 22%	'01 - 47%	'01 - 29%	'01 - 2%	'01 - *
36. Large corporations.	'02 – 2%	'02 – 17%	'02 – 65%	'02 – 14%	'02 – 1%
37. The United States Military.	'02 – 24%	'02 – 46%	'02 – 26%	'02 – 4%	'02 – 1%
	'01 - 25%	'01 - 50%	'01 - 24%	'01 - 1%	'01 - *
38. The federal government.	'02 – 7%	'02 – 44%	'02 – 45%	'02 – 3%	'02 - *
	'01 - 10%	'01 - 50%	'01 - 38%	'01 - 2%	'01 - *
	'00 - 4%	'00 - 32%	'00 - 56%	'00 - 8%	'00 - *
39. The media.	'02 – 1%	'02 – 11%	'02 – 60%	'02 – 27%	'02 – 1%
40. The United States Congress.	'02 – 9%	'02 – 43%	'02 – 44%	'02 – 3%	'02 – 1%
	'01 - 11%	'01 - 51%	'01 - 36%	'01 - 2%	'01 - *
41. Government workers.	'02 – 5%	'02 – 41%	'02 – 51%	'02 – 3%	'02 – 1%
42. Your local Member of Congress serving in Washington.	'02 – 9%	'02 – 43%	'02 – 40%	'02 – 4%	'02 – 4%
	'01 - 12%	'01 - 48%	'01 - 31%	'01 - 3%	'01 - 5%
	'00 - 8%	'00 - 43%	'00 - 42%	'00 - 5%	'00 - 3%

Now I am going to read a list of statements about politics and public service provided by college students. After I read each one, please tell me whether you strongly agree with the statement, somewhat agree with the statement, somewhat disagree with the statement, or strongly disagree with the statement. Here is the first one:

[ROTATE QUESTIONS]	STRONG-LY AGREE	SOME-WHAT AGREE	NET: AGREE	SOME-WHAT DISAGREE	STRON G-LY DISAGR EE	NET: DISAGR EE	DK/ REFUSED
43. I feel like I need more practical information about politics before I get involved.	'02 – 52% '01 - 43% '00 - 49%	'02 – 34% '01 - 40% '00 - 38%	'02 – 86% '01 - 83% '00 - 87%	'02 – 10% '01 - 13% '00 - 9%	'02 – 4% '01 - 4% '00 - 3%	'02 – 14% '01 - 17% '00 - 12%	'02 - * '01 - * '00 - 1%
44. Elected officials seem to be motivated by selfish reasons.	'02 – 20% '01 - 20% '00 - 27%	'02 – 47% '01 - 46% '00 - 47%	'02 – 67% '01 - 66% '00 - 74%	'02 – 27% '01 - 25% '00 - 22%	'02 – 5% '01 - 9% '00 - 3%	'02 – 32% '01 - 34% '00 - 25%	'02 - 1% '01 - 1% '00 - 1%
45. Politics is not relevant to my life right now.	'02 – 15% '01 - 7% '00 - 11%	'02 – 22% '01 - 16% '00 - 21%	'02 – 37% '01 - 23% '00 - 32%	'02 – 28% '01 - 26% '00 - 30%	'02 – 35% '01 - 51% '00 - 38%	'02 – 63% '01 - 77% '00 - 68%	'02 - *% '01 - * '00 - *
46.A I feel like I probably volunteer more of my time for political causes than most college students do. (n=600)	'02 – 7%	'02 – 17%	'02 – 23%	'02 – 31%	'02 – 45%	'02 – 76%	'02 – 1%
46.B I feel like I probably volunteer more of my time for community activities than most college students do. (n=600)	'02 – 18%	'02 – 32%	'02 – 50%	'02 – 31%	'02 – 18%	'02 – 49%	'02 – 1%
47. Volunteering in the community is easier than volunteering in politics.	'02 - 56% '01 - 40% '00 - 54%	'02 - 33% '01 - 41% '00 - 32%	'02 - 89% '01 - 81% '00 - 86%	'02 - 7% '01 - 12% '00 - 8%	'02 - 3% '01 - 5% '00 - 3%	'02 - 10% '01 - 17% '00 - 11%	'02 - 1% '01 - 2% '00 - 3%
48. Political involvement rarely has any tangible results.[3]	'02 - 8% '01 - 6% '00 - 10%	'02 - 34% '01 - 37% '00 - 41%	'02 - 42% '01 - 43% '00 - 51%	'02 - 39% '01 - 40% '00 - 35%	'02 - 17% '01 - 16% '00 - 13%	'02 - 56% '01 - 56% '00 - 48%	'02 - 2% '01 - 1% '00 - 3%

[3] Question wording was changed in 2002 - the previous wording was "Political involvement rarely has any immediate tangible results."

Now I am going to read another list. This list, also compiled by students, describes ways to get college students more involved in politics and public service. After I read each one, please tell me whether you think each would be a very effective, somewhat effective, not very effective, or not at all effective way to get college students more involved in politics and public service.

[ROTATE QUESTIONS]	VERY EFFECT-IVE	S'WHAT EFFECT-IVE	NET: EFFECT-IVE	NOT VERY EFFECT-IVE	NOT AT ALL EFFECT-IVE	NET: NOT EFFECT-IVE	DK/ REFUSED
49. If Federal and state governments offered loan forgiveness or signing bonuses to qualified students who commit to government work for a period of 3 to 5 years after college.	'02 – 45% '01 - 51% '00 - 45%	'02 – 46% '01 - 41% '00 - 43%	'02 – 91% '01 - 92% '00 - 88%	'02 - 6% '01 - 5% '00 - 10%	'02 - 2% '01 - 2% '00 - 2%	'02 – 8% '01 - 7% '00 - 12%	'02 - 1% '01 - * '00 - *
50. If more musicians, actors and sports figures that I respect were involved in politics or public service.	'02 – 22%	'02 – 49%	'02 – 71%	'02 – 20%	'02 – 9%	'02 – 29%	'02 - *
51. If students had direct contact with more elected officials, members of government, political candidates, campaigns and institutions.	'02 – 44% '01 - 46% '00 - 54%	'02 – 47% '01 - 46% '00 - 32%	'02 – 92% '01 - 92% '00 - 94%	'02 - 6% '01 - 7% '00 - 5%	'02 - 2% '01 - * '00 - *	'02 – 8% '01 - 8% '00 - 5%	'02 - * '01 - * '00 - *
52. If as part of the curriculum, colleges and universities created partnerships with local and state governments and offered academic credit to students who actively participated in public service activities.	'02 – 48% '01 - 53% '00 - 56%	'02 – 45% '01 - 41% '00 - 39%	'02 – 93% '01 - 94% '00 - 95%	'02 - 5% '01 - 4% '00 - 4%	'02 - 2% '01 - 1% '00 - 1%	'02 – 6% '01 - 5% '00 - 5%	'02 - 1% '01 - * '00 - *
53. If high schools offered opportunities for students to get involved in politics or public service in exchange for academic credit.	'02 – 53%	'02 – 41%	'02 – 93%	'02 - 5%	'02 - 2%	'02 – 6%	'02 - *
54. If government agencies and political organizations recruited students at campus job fairs like other industries.	'02 – 34%	'02 – 56%	'02 – 90%	'02 - 7%	'02 - 2%	'02 – 9%	'02 - *
55. If I knew that political or public service work would be considered favorably by graduate schools for admissions or by employers for hiring.	'02 – 44%	'02 – 48%	'02 – 92%	'02 - 5%	'02 - 2%	'02 – 8%	'02 - *
56. If there were more TV shows and movies like the West Wing that makes politics and public service seem interesting.	'02 – 18%	'02 – 45%	'02 – 63%	'02 – 26%	'02 – 10%	'02 – 36%	'02 - 1%

Now I am going to ask you a few questions about current events.

57. In general, would you say things in the country are headed in the right direction, or are they off on the wrong track?

	2002
Right direction	45%
Wrong track	44%
Mixed [VOL]	7%
Don't know	4%

58. Thinking about national issues for a moment, can you please tell me which issue concerns you most?

	2002	2001	2000
Iraq	25%	*	–
Net: Terrorism/National Security	33%	68%	
Terrorism		31%	–
Afghanistan/War on Terrorism		22%	–
Anthrax/Bio/Chemical Warfare		8%	
National Security		5%	
Foreign Affairs		3%	4%
Jobs and the economy	7%	4%	6%
Education	7%	5%	15%
Environment	1%	2%	5%
Crime (non-terrorist related)	2%	*	10%
Health care	1%	1%	5%
Other	17%	43%	
Don't know	4%	12%	

59. Which of the following statements comes closest to your own view:

	2002
The U.S. should take military action against Iraq if the United Nations is not allowed to conduct effective weapons inspections.	18%
The U.S. should take military action against Iraq if the United Nations is not allowed to conduct effective weapons inspections–but only with the support from its allies in the United Nations.	51%
The U.S. should not take military action against Iraq.	28%
Don't know	4%

60. How concerned are you about the possibility there will be more major terrorist attacks in the United States? Is that something that worries you a great deal, somewhat, not too much, or not at all?

	2002	2001	2001 (ABC News, 18+)
A great deal	27%	27%	36%
Somewhat	42%	46%	43%
Not too much	24%	21%	14%
Not at all	6%	6%	9%
Don't know	*	–	–

Thinking now about September 11th:

61. How much did the September 11th terrorist attacks affect how you think about politics and national issues?

	2002
A great deal	41%
Some	41%
Not much	14%
Not at all	3%
Don't know	1%

Moving on now:

62. Do you support or oppose reinstating the military draft? PROBE: Do you strongly or somewhat (CHOICE)?

	2002	2001
Strongly support	7%	8%
Somewhat support	22%	22%
Somewhat oppose	28%	26%
Strongly oppose	39%	42%
Don't know	5%	2%

63. If the draft were reinstated and you were selected—would you eagerly serve, serve with reservation, or would you try to seek an alterative?

	2002	2001
Eagerly serve	24%	29%
Serve with reservation	28%	31%
Seek an alternative	44%	38%
Don't know/Refused	3%	2%

64. When it comes to your feelings about being an American, do you consider yourself very patriotic, somewhat patriotic, not very patriotic, or not at all patriotic?

	2002	2001
Very patriotic	33%	48%
Somewhat patriotic	57%	44%
Not very patriotic	8%	6%
Not at all patriotic	2%	1%
Don't know/Refused	*	-

65. Please rate our political system on a scale from 0 to 10, where 0 means "deeply
flawed" and 10 means "very sound."

	2002
Net: Flawed (0-2)	3%
Deeply flawed (0)	2%
(1)	1%
(2)	1%
Net: (3-7)	69%
(3)	3%
(4)	5%
(5)	14%
(6)	17%
(7)	30%
Net: Sound (8-10)	26%
(8)	19%
(9)	5%
Very sound (10)	2%
Don't Know	1%
Mean	6.43

66. Not including sports or entertainment, approximately how often do you read a
newspaper on watch news related to current events? Would you say it is daily,

more than once per week, about once per week, a few times per month, about once per month, a few times per year, or less than once per year?

	2002
Daily	42%
More than once per week	29%
About once per week	15%
Few times per month	6%
About once per month	4%
Few times per year	3%
Don't know	1%

67. Approximately how often do you discuss politics and current events with your friends or family members? Would you say it is more than once per week, about once per week, a few times per month, about once per month, a few times per year, or less than once per year?

	2002	2001
More than once per week	37%	58%
About once per week	31%	25%
Few times per month	15%	12%
About once per month	8%	3%
Few times per year	4%	2%
Less than once per year	4%	*
Don't know	1%	

68. Growing up, approximately how often would you say your parents discussed politics and current events with you at home? Would you say it was more than once per week, about once per week, a few times per month, about once per month, a few times per year, or less than once per year?

	2002	2001
More than once per week	28%	32%
About once per week	18%	21%
Few times per month	19%	24%

About once per month	13%	10%
Few times per year	11%	8%
Less than once per year	10%	5%
Don't know	1%	*

69. Have you ever met or had contact with a political candidate or elected official (local, state or federally elected) that is not a member of your family?

	2002	2001	2000
Yes	59%	71%	66%
No	40%	29%	34%

70. While in high school, did you volunteer for community service or not?

	2002
Yes	80%
No	20%

71. **[IF YES IN Q 70]** Was community service required by your school, were there incentives provided–or was it completely voluntary?

	2002
Required	23%
Incentives	13%
Completely voluntary	63%

72. How often, if ever, do you watch the TV show–The West Wing–often sometimes, rarely, or never?

	2002
Often	4%
Sometimes	9%
Rarely	16%
Never	70%

The following questions are for statistical purposes only:

73. Currently, do you work full-time, part-time, during the summer only, or not at all?

	2002	2001
Full-time	6%	8%
Part-time	45%	47%
Summer only	32%	34%
Not at all	16%	11%

74. Which of the following best describes the area where you go to school–a city of 100,000 or more, a suburb of a city of 100,000 or more, a small city, a town or, a rural area?

	2002	2001
City of 100,000 or more	31%	38%
Suburb	11%	11%
Small city	33%	37%
Town	15%	10%
Rural area	9%	3%
Don't know/Refused	1%	1%

75. In which year of college are you?

	2002	2001	2000
First/Freshman	31%	32%	29%
Second/Sophomore	23%	24%	24%
Third/Junior	20%	20%	19%
Fourth/Senior	23%	22%	24%
Fifth	4%	3%	4%

76. Please indicate your race:

	2002	2001	2000
White	72%	80%	78%
African American	14%	8%	9%
Hispanic	7%	5%	4%
Asian	6%	3%	4%
Native American	1%	1%	2%
Other	1%	2%	2%
Refused	*	1%	2%

77. For tabulation purposes only, please tell me which of the following income categories includes your parents' total household income for 2001–just stop me when I read the correct category…

	2002	2001
Less than $20,000	6%	3%
$20,000-$29,999	8%	4%
$30,000-$39,999	12%	9%
$40,000-$49,999	12%	11%
$50,000-$74,999	20%	21%
$75,000-$99,999	14%	18%
$100,000 or over	14%	24%
Don't know/Refused	15%	10%

78. **[IF REFUSED]** Well, can you just tell me whether the total income is below $50,000 or $50,000 or above?

	2002	2001
Below $50,000	16%	11%
$50,000 or above	24%	45%
Still refused	60%	43%

79. Which one of these best describes your religious preferences: Fundamentalist or Evangelical Christian, mainstream Protestant, Catholic, Jewish, some other religion, or no religious preference?

	2002
Fundamentalist or Evangelical Christian	24%
Protestant-mainstream	15%
Catholic	24%
Jewish	1%
Other	21%
No preference	14%
Refused	1%

80. **[IF FUNDAMENTALIST/EVANGELICAL or PROTESTANT]** Do you consider yourself a born-again Christian, or not?

	2002
Yes	50%
No	48%
Refused	2%

81. Do you regularly attend religious services?

	2002
Yes	51%
No	49%
Refused	*

82. Code Gender.

	2002	2001	2000
Male	50%	50%	50%
Female	50%	50%	50%

83. Do you attend a public or private institution?

	2002
Public	75%
Private	25%

84. Recode: Region where institution is located.

	2002	2000
East/Northeast	15%	11%
Midwest	27%	35%
South	39%	41%
West	19%	13%

Notes

Preface:

[i] Institute of Politics Survey of Student Attitudes, October 2002

[ii] "Voluntcerism, Education, and the Shadow of September Eleventh," Leon and Sylvia Panetta Institute for Public Policy, May 2002

[iii] Ibid.

[iv] "Young Americans' Call to Public Service." Hart-Teeter Study for the Council for Excellence in Government. May 2002

[v] "Volunteerism, Education, and the Shadow of September Eleventh," Leon and Sylvia Panetta Institute for Public Policy, May 2002

Chapter 1: Ruby Tuesday

[vi] www.september11news.com

Chapter 2: A Generation Responds

[vii] *Newsweek*, "Generation 9/11," 11/12/01

[viii] Adam S. Kirby, "From ashes of tragedy comes Generation 9/11," *The Marquette Tribune*, 11/16/01

[ix] "Volunteerism, Education, and the Shadow of September Eleventh," Panetta Institute for Public Policy. May 2002.

[x] Campus Attitudes on Politics and Public Survey. Harvard University, Institute of Politics, 2000.

[xi] "Volunteerism, Education, and the Shadow of September Eleventh," Panetta Institute for Public Policy. May 2002."

[xii] Office of Alabama Secretary of State Jim Bennett, press release, 2/19/99.

xiii Burke, John P. "The Institutional Presidency." In "The Presidency and the Political System." Ed. Michael Nelson. Washington: CQ Press, 2000.

xiv Institute of Politics Survey of Student Attitudes, October 2002.

xv Interview with Robert Putnam. March 21, 2002.

xvi Center for Information & Research on Civic Learning and Engagement Survey, University of Maryland. January 2002.

Chapter 3: Insecurity

xvii "Frequently Asked Questions About the War on Terrorism at Home and Abroad." The White House. Accessed 14 March 2002. www.whitehouse.gov/response/faq-homeland.html

xviii "Hundreds in Michigan Asked to Submit to 'Terror Questioning'." CNN.com. 28 November 2001. Accessed 20 March 2002. http://www.cnn.com/2001/US/11/27/inv.michigan.interviews/index.html

xix Blacks for Profiling." The National Review. 6 February 2002. Accessed 20 March 2002. http://www.nationalreview.com/comment/comment-levy020602.shtml

xx "Bush Bashes INS Over Hijackers' Visas." USA TODAY. 13 March 2002. Accessed 20 March 2002. http://story.news.yahoo.com/news?tmpl=story&u=/usatoday/20020314/ts_usatoday/3940023

xxi "INS in New Visa Row." CNN.Com. 23 March 2002. Accessed 20 March 2002. http://www.cnn.com/2002/US/03/23/ins.pakistanis/index.html

xxii "Senate Passes Border Bill" Associated Press. 18 April 2002. Accessed 23 April, 2002. http://story.news.yahoo.com/news?tmpl=story&u=/ap/20020419/ap_on_go_co/border_security_26

Chapter 4: Guns and Butter

xxiii Kaminski, Matthew. "Anti-Terrorism Requires Nation Building". *Wall Street Journal*.15 March, 2002 A10.

xxiv Ibid.

xxv "Youth's propensity responses do not distinguish between enlistment and entering the military as an officer (or officer-trainee)" (YATS 1998, 75).

xxvi Wilson, Michael J. et al. *Youth Attitude Tracking Study 1998: Propensity and Advertising Report*. (Rockville: Westat, Inc., 2000), 75.

xxvii Ibid.

xxviii Hochberg, Lee (interviewer). "The Selling of the Army" in *NewsHour* with Col. Lisle Brook.

xxix Ibid.

xxx Harris Interactive Survey. Rochester: New York, 28 September 2001.
<http://www.harrisinteractive.com/news/newscats.asp?NewsID=366>, (cited 18 April 2002).

xxxi Kirk, Jeremy. "At Manhattan Recruiting Center, Attacks Pique Enlistment Interest." *Stars and Stripes.* 22 Sept. 2001.
< http://ww2.pstripes.osd.mil/01/sep01/ed092201k.html>. (cited 20 April 2002).
xxxii Ibid.

xxxiii Harris Interactive Survey. Rochester: New York, 28 September 2001.
<http://www.harrisinteractive.com/news/newscats.asp?NewsID=366>, (cited 18 April 2002).

xxxiv *Young America: Life After 9/11 Poll.* The Observer Dispatch 2002.
<http://www.uticaod.com/youth/poll/poll.htm>. (cited 19 April 2002).

xxxv Cooper, Jen. "Pacifists Are Filing for CO Status in Growing Numbers." *Scripps Howard Foundation Wire.* Washington, D.C.
<http://www.shfwire.com/story.phtml?action=show_story&id=371>. (cited 18 April 2002).

xxxvi Ibid.

xxxvii Marquardt, Katy. "College Campuses Hold Peace Rallies." *Scripps Howard Foundation Wire.* Washington, D.C.
<http://www.shfwire.com/story.phtml?action=show_story&id=371>. (cited 18 April 2002).

xxxviii Ibid.

xxxix Moore, David W. "Gallup Poll Analyses: Military and Foreign Policy Issues Fade Among Public's Priorities but Terrorism Still Number-one Issue." *Gallup News Service.* Princeton, NJ. 21 January 2002.
<http://www.udel.edu/global/agenda/2002/readings/gallupjanuary%20poll.html>. (cited 20 April 2002).

Chapter 5: An Emerging Agenda

xl Wall Street Journal 15 March 91

xli Testimony of chairman Representative Christopher H. Smith at the Subcommittee of International Operations and Human Rights hearing on "United Nations Peacekeeping." 20 September 2000.

xlii Ibid.

xliii *An Introduction to United Nations Peacekeeping.*
http://www.un.org/Depts/dpko/dpko/intro/intro.htm . 13 March 2002.